Praise for *The Best American Poetry*

"Each year, a vivid snapshot of what a distinguished poet finds exciting, fresh, and memorable: and over the years, as good a comprehensive overview of contemporary poetry as there can be."

—Robert Pinsky

"*The Best American Poetry* series has become one of the mainstays of the poetry publication world. For each volume, a guest editor is enlisted to cull the collective output of large and small literary journals published that year to select seventy-five of the year's 'best' poems. The guest editor is also asked to write an introduction to the collection, and the anthologies would be indispensable for these essays alone; combined with [David] Lehman's 'state-of-poetry' forewords and the guest editors' introductions, these anthologies seem to capture the zeitgeist of the current attitudes in American poetry."

—Academy of American Poets

"A high volume of poetic greatness . . . in all of these volumes . . . there is brilliance, there is innovation, there are surprises."

—*The Villager*

"A year's worth of the very best!"

—*People*

"A preponderance of intelligent, straightforward poems."

—*Booklist*

"Certainly it attests to poetry's continuing vitality."

—*Publishers Weekly* (starred review)

"A 'best' anthology that really lives up to its title."

—*Chicago Tribune*

"An essential purchase."

—*The Washington Post*

"For the small community of American poets, the *Best American Poetry* is the *Michelin Guide*, the *Reader's Digest*, and the Prix Goncourt."

—*L'Observateur*

OTHER VOLUMES IN THIS SERIES

THE
BEST
AMERICAN
POETRY
2018

◊ ◊ ◊

Dana Gioia, Editor

David Lehman, Series Editor

SCRIBNER POETRY

NEW YORK LONDON TORONTO SYDNEY NEW DELHI

Scribner Poetry
An Imprint of Simon & Schuster, Inc.
1230 Avenue of the Americas
New York, NY 10020

First Scribner edition September 2018

SCRIBNER POETRY and design are registered trademarks of The Gale Group, Inc., used under license by Simon & Schuster, Inc., the publisher of this work.

For information about special discounts for bulk purchases, please contact Simon & Schuster Special Sales at 1-866-506-1949 or business@simonandschuster.com.

The Simon & Schuster Speakers Bureau can bring authors to your live event. For more information or to book an event, contact the Simon & Schuster Speakers Bureau at 1-866-248-3049 or visit our website at www.simonspeakers.com.

Manufactured in the United States of America

3   5   7   9   10   8   6   4   2

Library of Congress Control Number: 88644281

ISBN 978-1-5011-2779-3
ISBN 978-1-5011-2780-9 (pbk)
ISBN 978-1-5011-2781-6 (ebook)

CONTENTS

David Lehman was born in New York City. Educated at Stuyvesant High School and Columbia University, he spent two years as a Kellett Fellow at Clare College, Cambridge, and worked as Lionel Trilling's research assistant upon his return from England. *Poems in the Manner Of* (2017), his most recent book, comprises poems written in imitation, appreciation, translation, or parody of poets from Catullus to Charles Bukowski. His eight earlier collections include *New and Selected Poems* (2013), *When a Woman Loves a Man* (2005), and *The Daily Mirror: A Journal in Poetry* (2000), all from Scribner. He is the editor of *The Oxford Book of American Poetry* (Oxford, 2006) and *Great American Prose Poems: From Poe to the Present* (Scribner, 2003), among other anthologies. Two prose books recently appeared: *The State of the Art: A Chronicle of American Poetry, 1988–2014* (Pittsburgh), containing all the forewords he had written to date for *The Best American Poetry*, and *Sinatra's Century: One Hundred Notes on the Man and His World* (HarperCollins). *A Fine Romance: Jewish Songwriters, American Songs* (Schocken) won the Deems Taylor Award from the American Society of Composers, Authors, and Publishers (ASCAP) in 2010. Lehman lives in New York City and in Ithaca, New York.

FOREWORD

by David Lehman

◊　◊　◊

In 2017 one former guest editor of *The Best American Poetry* succeeded another when Kevin Young (*BAP 2011*) was hired to take the place of Paul Muldoon (*BAP 2005*) as poetry editor of *The New Yorker*. Paul, who continues to teach at Princeton, is the coauthor, with Jean Hanff Korelitz, of a critically acclaimed re-creation of the holiday feast in James Joyce's "The Dead." And for the first time in a decade, he is eligible to grace *The New Yorker* with a poetic tour de force on the order of "Aubade," which ran in the January 29, 2018, issue.

As for Kevin, he left his post at Emory University to head the Schomburg Center for Research in Black Culture in New York City, where his first public appearances celebrated the Schomburg's acquisition of James Baldwin's archives ("a well-timed coup," said *The New York Times*) and the life and legacy of tenor saxophonist Sonny Rollins, who used to practice on New York's Williamsburg Bridge (because no one complained about the noise) and for whom the bridge may someday be named.

For an admiring profile of Kevin Young that ran in *Esquire*, Robert Baird asked David Remnick, the editor of *The New Yorker*, who hired Young, why *The New Yorker* "still publishes poems," as if that were a quixotic or archaic thing to do. "Poetry is arguably, in some compressed and magical fashion, the highest form of expression, the greatest devotion we have to our most intricate invention, language itself," Remnick wrote in an email. "How can we publish a magazine that proposes to be literary, as well as journalistic, that does not publish poetry?"[1]

The title *Esquire*'s editors affixed to Baird's piece—"Can Kevin

---

1. Robert P. Baird, "Can Kevin Young Make Poetry Matter Again?," *Esquire*, November 6, 2017, at http://www.esquire.com/entertainment/a13135556/kevin-young-poetry/.

Young Make Poetry Matter Again?"—echoes that of the essay Dana Gioia wrote for *The Atlantic* in 1991: "Can Poetry Matter?" In reaction to this echo, one can 1) revert to adage (*plus ça change, plus c'est la même chose*), or 2) exclaim over the persistence of the worry, which seems to have outlived the related anxiety that either the novel or the author is dead, or 3) linger over some paradoxes. Perhaps never before have so many people written poetry despite the universally acknowledged truth that few folks buy poetry books. "It is almost eerie, the number of people who want to be poets," Louise Glück remarked when working on *The Best American Poetry 1993*, and the number has gone up in the twenty-five years since. An academic industry has grown around the teaching of poetry and other forms of creative writing, yet voices keep proclaiming that poetry is ready for the morgue, has forfeited its public responsibility, has lost its audience, has slid into irrelevance. A survey released by the National Endowment for the Arts in 2015 provides statistics to back up the gloom-and-doomsayers out there. If your idea of an active public is anyone who has read "at least one poem" in a calendar year, that public declined precipitously in the ten-year period ending in 2012 and is limited to 6.7 percent of the population. Do the math and you still get a hefty number of people—until you remind yourself of how broad the category is and how low the figure would be if people were asked to name a living poet or to recite a couple of lines of verse.

Robert Baird, author of the *Esquire* piece, has written one of the most cogent critiques of, or laments for, poetry today. (There are plenty of bad ones.) "Spend It All" appeared on the *Best American Poetry* blog on January 13, 2012. The post begins with an arresting observation: "Pass much time in the company of poets—young or old, online or off—and soon enough you'll find yourself privy to the cycles of consternation and dismay inspired by the general insignificance of poetry." This is undeniable even if one reflexively counters with the observation that America can now boast of having more poets per capita than ever in its history. Poetry has "slipped beyond decadence" into an eccentricity. "Poetry lost the common reader a long time ago, if it ever had her, and from where I sit, it seems well on its way to losing the uncommon reader as well," Baird writes. "Time was you had to know at least a little Larkin or Lowell or Creeley to count yourself a cultured intellectual, just as older times demanded you had to keep current with opera and ballet. No more. These days we feel like we're shouldering our share of the civilizational burden if we keep up our subscription to

The New York Times and pledge yearly to NPR." It sounds despairing, but Baird keeps his cool. "If you're a poet you decide that there are too many poems that need writing, far too many that need reading. Plus, you figure, if people don't like poetry, then bully for them, just like Frank O'Hara said all those years ago. Poetry, like virtue, is its own reward." Then, too, he concludes, with the fortitude of Tennyson's Ulysses, there is such a thing as "literary magnificence."[2]

Everyone has always wanted to be a poet. The desire to write poetry, to live the life of a poet, has a long and honorable tradition. Here, from "The Fall of Hyperion," is Keats's statement of the theme:

> Who alive can say,
> "Thou art no Poet; may'st not tell thy dreams?"
> Since every man whose soul is not a clod
> Hath visions, and would speak, if he had loved
> And been well nurtured in his mother tongue.
> Whether the dream now purpos'd to rehearse
> Be poet's or fanatic's will be known
> When this warm scribe my hand is in the grave.

Keats anticipated Freud, who established the rationale for the argument that there is a poet in each of us. If the unconscious is the true genius, if it is the source of the dreams, the errors, and the jokes that prefigure poems, then all who dream, who err, who jest can get into the action in this game that has few and mostly lenient referees, and what's the harm? If there is even a slim chance that the amateur poet, the student poet, the Sunday poet may participate in the cultural heritage that nourishes the imagination and resists the mighty forces of materialism, isn't that all the justification we need to encourage the multitudes to write poetry and prose?

There is a flip side. Lack of talent or inspiration hasn't stopped a lot of Shagpats from getting in on the action.[3] A good heart and the power

2. Robert P. Baird, "Spend It All," *Best American Poetry* blog, January 13, 2012, at http://blog.bestamericanpoetry.com/the_best_american_poetry/2012/01/spend-it-all-by-robert-p-baird.html.

3. Shagpat is the tyrant whose power inheres in his hair in George Meredith's novel *The Shaving of Shagpat*. "Rhyme removed, much ethereal music leaps up from the word, music which has hitherto chirped unnoticed in the expanse of prose. Any rhyme forbidden, many Shagpats were unwigged."—T. S. Eliot, "Reflections on Vers Libres" (1917).

of positive thinking can take the poetaster a long way. Social media accelerate the tendency. The queen of Instagram poets is Rupi Kaur, a Canadian woman born in India. She has two books and 1.5 million followers on Instagram. She also has cash customers. Two and a half million copies of *Milk and Honey*, her first book, have been sold. Her poems, signed with her name in lowercase, are sincere, well-meaning, and sensitive in the approved way of greeting card verse. According to *New York* magazine, Queen Rupi reigns in "the realm of college freshwomen who have recently been or may soon go through break-ups." Carl Wilson of *The New York Times* defines her target audience as consisting of readers "who may think of poetry as the literary equivalent of opera or ballet, a privileged-white-male establishment hostile to their interests." Covering the "inevitable backlash against Instagram's favourite poet" for *The Guardian*, Priya Khaira-Hanks writes that Kaur and some of her rivals "hit upon a winning formula: rupturing short confessional pieces with erratic line breaks to share hard-won truths." Example: "if you are not enough for yourself / you will never be enough / for someone else." In *The Wall Street Journal*, the headline of Nina Sovich's piece on the Rupi Kaur phenomenon—which lacked a single line of Kaur's poetry—summed it up. "My Love Is Like a Hashtag: 'Instagram Poets' Sell Well."[4] The last best defense of such verse is that it may serve as a "gateway" to the real stuff. I can give lip service to this proposition even as I note that it sometimes seems as if the only time articles about poetry appear prominently in the culture pages of our newspapers is when the subject is a counterfeit, the implication being that we'd be prepared to embrace poetry if only it weren't poetry.

Just as it occurs to me that the self-delete function of Snapchat may make it an exemplary medium, Mark Bibbins lets me know that William Carlos Williams's "This Is Just to Say" has become "a meme on Twitter, with people posting parodies/variations—some of which are receiving thousands of likes/retweets." In Williams's sly poem the

4. Carl Wilson, "Why Rupi Kaur and Her Peers Are the Most Popular Poets in the World," *The New York Times*, December 15, 2017; Nina Sovich, "My Love Is Like a Hashtag: 'Instagram Poets' Sell Well," *The Wall Street Journal*, September 11, 2017; Priya Khaira-Hanks, "Rupi Kaur: The Inevitable Backlash Against Instagram's Favourite Poet," *The Guardian*, October 4, 2017. The only lines of verse quoted in Nina Sovich's "My Love Is Like a Hashtag" were "Love made / her wild" by Thom Young, apparently a swipe at the pseudonymous Atticus, author of *Love Her Wild* (Atria Books).

speaker confesses to eating the plums in the icebox that "you" were planning to have for breakfast. "Forgive me" he says, but what follows sounds more like a gloat than an apology. The plums, he explains, were delicious, "so sweet and so cold." Kenneth Koch, a master parodist, took Williams's formula to a logical extreme in four "variations." The last of the four epitomizes the comic sublime, packing an exclamatory surprise in each line: "Last night we went dancing and I broke your leg. / Forgive me. I was clumsy, / And I wanted you here in the wards, where I am the doctor!"

I have used the fake apology as a prompt in my classes at the New School and in the weekly "Next Line, Please" challenges on the website of *The American Scholar*, so it didn't altogether surprise me to learn that the fake apology was causing a Twitter ruckus. Many of the entries, seemingly composed off the cuff, turned the case of the eaten plums into new lyrics for familiar poems or jingles in the public domain. A writer self-characterized as "Medusa without frontiers" and "Ophelia in waders" opted for an Emily Dickinson locution: "Because I would not stop for plums, / I ate all yours, you see. / And now the icebox holds just pits; / I'm sorry.—Willie C." Sir Ian modeled his entry on the opening of Allen Ginsberg's "Howl": "I saw the best plums of my generation destroyed by Williams, starving hysterical naked, / dragging himself through the icebox shelves at dawn looking for a sweet cold fix."[5]

You may say: If this is poetry, what happened to language charged with meaning? Where are the best words in the best order? Is this what Wallace Stevens had in mind when he wrote that poetry is "a means of redemption," "a search for the inexplicable," "the renovation of experience," and, just to keep you on your toes, "a pheasant disappearing in the bush"? Does this do what Emily Dickinson prescribed—take the top of your head off? The prosecution rests.

In chambers, the judge reminds counsel that the gallant thing is to change the subject and end the paragraph on a positive note. And the jury is addressed as one poet talking to another, trying to define the indefinable. Though judgment is subjective, and rankings are best left to posterity, the inevitably unsuccessful attempt to define poetry can help us to grasp its essence and recognize the genuine article when it comes along. "Poetry is language that sounds better and means more," in Charles Wright's formulation. "Poetry is philosophy's sister, the

---

5. MedusaSansFrontières, OpheliaInWaders, and IanWhittington, @Sir__ Ian, are the Twitter handles.

one that wears makeup," says Jennifer Grotz. Paradoxes please us: "a poem is an interruption of silence, whereas prose is a continuation of noise" (Billy Collins). Poetry is a game—and it is also a lover's quarrel with the world of words. Then it occurs to me: substitute "America" or "paradise" for "poetry" in that formulation, and the game gets even more interesting. America is a melting pot, or it's the land of the free agent. Paradise is always being lost or maybe it's a version of the place where, when you have to go there, they have to take you in. Poetry is a café, or it's the place where parallel lines cross, or up close it's the gibbous mirrored eye of an insect.

★ ★ ★

Dana Gioia and I have been friends since we met in 1982. I know of no one more dedicated to literature and the arts in the largest sense: he loves to read and talk about poetry, and he is equally passionate and knowing about theater, opera, jazz, and painting. After a fling at Harvard as a graduate student in literature, Dana went to business school at Stanford and joined the ranks of maverick poets who earned their living in business or a profession rather than in academe. By day he worked for General Foods, but he managed to publish poems and ambitious essays in magazines such as *The Hudson Review*. He became a leader of the New Formalism, a movement determined to restore to poetry the importance formerly placed on rhyme, meter, and traditional form. He also translated Montale, helped make the case for the underrated Weldon Kees, and wrote touching personal memoirs about Elizabeth Bishop (whom he had come to know while at Harvard) and John Cheever.

After giving up his business career to give more time to the literary life, Dana wrote poems and essays and opera libretti, edited textbooks and anthologies, translated Seneca, collaborated with all sorts of folks on all sorts of worthy projects. But he had another surprise in store for us. In 2003 he became the chairman of the National Endowment for the Arts, in which capacity he served for six years. When he took the helm, the organization was in bad odor. In a burst of energy he refashioned its image and resuscitated its reputation. He launched initiatives to enlarge the readership for serious literature ("The Big Read"); to promote the memorization of verse ("Poetry Out Loud"); to provide "creative art therapy" to returning veterans ("Operation Homecoming"); to produce Shakespeare plays in untraditional venues, such as military bases; and to contrive new ways to celebrate our heroes of opera and jazz. And he managed to sell the arts to congressmen not necessarily disposed to be supportive.

It is safe to say that not since Archibald MacLeish headed the Library of Congress has a poet worked so hard, and accomplished so much of value, in so prominent a position in the federal government. Not everyone can see beyond his or her essential understanding of poetry to be able to acknowledge the legitimacy of rival conceptions. Dana has that ability and in this book has done his best to represent the remarkable variety to be found in American poetry at its best in 2018.

★　★　★

We lost two titans in 2017: at the age of ninety, John Ashbery died on September 3; Richard Wilbur passed on October 14, aged ninety-six.[6]

A graduate of Amherst College (class of 1942), Dick Wilbur served during World War II with the 36th Infantry Division. He saw action in Italy, France, and Germany. Upon his return he taught at his alma mater and at Harvard, Wellesley, Wesleyan, and Smith. He liked living in the country. With his wife, Charlee, to whom he was devoted, he lived in Cummington, Massachusetts, birthplace of William Cullen Bryant, and spent many springs in Key West, Florida. In 2004 his *Collected Poems 1943–2004* appeared from Harcourt. Twice he won the Pulitzer Prize. He wrote lyrics for Leonard Bernstein's *Candide*, and his translations from seventeenth-century French drama (Molière, Racine, Corneille) are performed widely. Wilbur's mastery of rhetoric and command of poetic form is or should be self-evident to all who have wrestled with words and their meanings. In his poems he weds deep humane intelligence with superb technique and unfailing fealty to the ideals of beauty and truth. "A poem should not be like a Double-Crostic; it should not be the sort of puzzle in which you get nothing until you get it all," he wrote. "Art does not or should not work that way; we are not cheated of a symphony if we fail to react to some passage on the flute, and a good poem should yield itself more than once, offering the reader an early and sure purchase, and deepening repeatedly as he comes to know it better."

Dick was the most genial and gracious of individuals. I profited from his expertise on many subjects: Edgar Allan Poe, the great American songbook, French classical tragedy, May Swenson, riddles, the haiku stanza

6. As we go to press, the sad news reaches me that Donald Hall died two days ago. In addition to all his other accomplishments, and there are many, Don served as the guest editor of *The Best American Poetry 1989*, the second volume in this series. He was a great friend and mentor, and his ideas and methods, based on years of experience as an anthologist, proved invaluable to me in subsequent years —DL, June 25, 2018

put to narrative or expository use. Twelve guest editors in this series have selected Wilbur's poems. His contributor's note in *The Best American Poetry 1999* concluded: "His several books for children have amused some adults." There then followed this comment on his poem "This Pleasing Anxious Being": "I think that people resist as long as they can a full sense of the world's change and of their own aging. At last, when a certain number of irreplaceable people are gone, and the home place has been razed, and one is the only rememberer of certain things, the gut acknowledges what the mind has always thought it knew. That is the source of this poem, which moves both back and forward in time, and considers time in a number of perspectives. The title is taken from the twenty-second stanza of Gray's 'Elegy Written in a Country Churchyard.'"

Three days before John Ashbery died, my wife and I saw *Marjorie Prime*, Michael Almereyda's latest movie, with an all-star cast (Jon Hamm, Geena Davis, Lois Smith) and wonderful samplings of a Beethoven string quartet, Poulenc, Mozart, "I Shall Be Released," and the dialogue of *Casablanca*. But the highlight of *Marjorie Prime* occurs when the character played by Tim Robbins reads aloud a love letter addressed to his mother-in-law, now deceased, said to have been written by a tennis-playing French-Canadian suitor who expresses the usual sentiments then abruptly switches to the first six lines of John Ashbery's "At North Farm":

> Somewhere someone is traveling furiously toward you,
> At incredible speed, traveling day and night,
> Through blizzards and desert heat, across torrents,
>   through narrow passes.
> But will he know where to find you,
> Recognize you when he sees you,
> Give you the thing he has for you?

I phoned John the next evening to tell him of our pleasure in hearing these lines. Aside from an intermittent cough, John sounded like John, and it gives me pleasure to report that he remained his witty, droll, clever, charming self right up to the end. A few days later I was writing copy in the past tense.

John was a mentor to me and a good friend. I went to readings he gave in my sophomore year at Columbia and was, like many of my classmates, blown away by his long poem "The Skaters," which many of my buddies on the *Columbia Review*, committed as we were to the aesthetic of the

New York School, thought was the single finest long poem in English since "The Waste Land." He very quickly became my favorite poet.

Some of his friends called him Ashes. I favored JA in part because of his brilliant early poem "The Picture of Little JA in a Prospect of Flowers," the title of which was itself a lift from a poem by Andrew Marvell. We—those of us privileged enough to get close to the man—would entertain one another with anecdotes about him, clever things he said, or just news of a great new poem, such as "Self-Portrait in a Convex Mirror," which knocked our socks off when it appeared in *Poetry* magazine in 1974. A year later it was the title poem of a poetry collection that went on to capture the Pulitzer Prize, the National Book Award, and the National Book Critics Circle Award, an unprecedented triple crown.

It was my great good luck that our professional paths crossed three significant times in the 1970s and 1980s. John and I shared an office at Brooklyn College the year I taught there. Later, when I reviewed books for *Newsweek*, John was the magazine's art critic. And when I launched *The Best American Poetry* series in 1988 with Scribner, JA was our first guest editor. So it was not only as a poet but also as a teacher, a critic, a journalist, and an editor that he inspired me.

My lifelong devotion to John's work is reflected in such publications as *Beyond Amazement: New Essays on John Ashbery* (1980) and *The Last Avant-Garde: The Making of the New York School of Poets* (1998). In 1984 Harvey Shapiro of *The New York Times Magazine* phoned and commissioned a profile for the magazine's "creative mind" series. I'm glad I got to interview him formally, though I never met anyone cagier; to simulate a conversation with him in public, which we did several times, required ingenuity and the willingness to look foolish. Sometimes things he said in interviews entered the general discourse. "Often people don't listen to you when you speak to them. It's only when you talk to yourself that they prick up their ears." And: "I am aware of the pejorative associations of the word 'escapist,' but I insist that we need all the escapism we can get and even that isn't going to be enough."

Strikingly different in many particulars, Ashbery and Wilbur have in common a profound understanding of English and American poetry as a living, constantly evolving thing with a great past that we can best cherish by treating it as part of our present. The poems of these exemplars will continue to nourish us for decades to come. Of few predictions can I be so confident.

Dana Gioia is a native Californian of Italian and Mexican descent. He received his BA and MBA from Stanford University and an MA in comparative literature from Harvard University. Gioia, who has served as chairman of the National Endowment for the Arts, is the author of five full-length collections of poetry, most recently *99 Poems: New & Selected*. Currently the Poet Laureate of California, he has written three opera libretti, edited anthologies, and translated poetry from Latin, Italian, and German. In 1991 his essay "Can Poetry Matter?" made a dent in the national consciousness. As chairman of the NEA, Gioia garnered bipartisan support in the United States Congress for public funding of the arts and arts education. (*Business Week* referred to him as "the man who saved the NEA.") "Poetry Out Loud," one of his several initiatives, involves nearly half a million high school students across the country in a national poetry recitation contest that awards $50,000 in scholarships. "Operation Homecoming" brought distinguished American authors to conduct workshops among troops returning from Iraq and Afghanistan. In 2011 Gioia became the Judge Widney Professor of Poetry and Public Culture at the University of Southern California, where he teaches each fall semester. He has received ten honorary degrees. He divides his time between Los Angeles and Sonoma County, California.

INTRODUCTION

by Dana Gioia

◇   ◇   ◇

American poetry is thriving. American poetry is in decline. The poetry audience has never been bigger. The audience has dropped to historic lows. The mass media ignores poetry. The media has rediscovered it. There have never been so many opportunities for poets. American poets find fewer options each year. The university provides a vibrant environment for poets. Academic culture has become stagnant and remote. Literary bohemias have been destroyed by gentrification and rising real estate prices. New bohemias have emerged across the nation. All of these contradictory statements are true, and all of them are false, depending on your point of view. The state of American poetry is a tale of two cities.

Consider the question of poetry's current audience. In traditional terms, poetry's audience has declined significantly in recent years. According to the massive Survey for Public Participation in the Arts conducted at five-year intervals by the National Endowment for the Arts, poetry readership dropped from 20 percent of the adult population in 1982 to nearly 7 percent in 2012. Poetry's slump matched a larger decline in all sorts of literary reading among every sector of the population. Poetry's situation seemed dire.

Cultural trends, however, are rarely linear. When things change, they often change direction. There was one odd statistic in the 2012 NEA poetry data, which was inconsistent with all the other measurements. The youngest group of adults (ages 18–24) read more poetry than any other segment. This result was puzzling because for years younger Americans read less of everything—poetry, fiction, books, magazines, newspapers—than older groups. No one much noticed the anomaly, even though American culture is often led by youth trends. Then in the next NEA report in 2017, national poetry readership nearly doubled to 12 percent. Poetry was suddenly a rapidly growing art form with 28 million adult readers. What was going on?

It was a tale of poetry's two overlapping cities—print versus performance. Culture is hard to measure in times of social and technological change. The NEA study measures conventional literary reading among American adults (print plus ebooks and text-based internet). It doesn't track anyone under eighteen. The survey also doesn't include poetry readings—live or in the media—as part of "literary reading." Meanwhile a huge cultural shift has occurred outside the scope of the survey among youth involved in performance and digital media. Technology has allowed poetry, which had begun in preliterate societies as a spoken art, to reconnect with its auditory origins. Print now coexists with other equally powerful media for poetry.

The chief way American poets now reach their audience is through readings, either live or transmitted by radio, television, and internet. The new venues, such as YouTube, haven't replaced print, but they have amplified it. The interest and excitement fostered by the new auditory culture has nurtured a new readership for print poetry. This trend has changed poetry culture, especially for young or emerging writers.

In a culture where elite journals such as *The Yale Review* or *The Hopkins Review* have circulation under a thousand copies, a teenager's homemade YouTube video with 1,100 hits may reach more "readers." Poetry performance is no longer confined to small, local events—a few poets reading in a half-empty café. Some slam poetry videos have reached millions of viewers. In a more academic context, four million teenagers have participated in "Poetry Out Loud," the national high school poetry recitation contest. Many of them film and post their performances. As the new NEA statistics suggest, the new and ubiquitous auditory media have helped increase poetry's print readership.

Spoken word and performance poetry don't replace written work. The new forms exist as alternative approaches to the same art—one focused on the page, the other on the stage. The different forms, however, influence each other. It is impossible to read new literary poems without noticing how much more important sound has become.

Younger poets have grown up hearing the beat, rhyme, and wordplay of hip-hop. They read their poems aloud to live audiences. They have also felt the power of oral poetry's self-presentation—a performer speaking directly to an audience. There is nothing surprising about the influence of the new forms of oral poetry. Spoken language constantly revitalizes the written word. Why else did Dante give up the prestige of Latin for the vulgar Italian tongue? Or Langston Hughes use the sounds of Harlem speech and sung blues?

If anyone doubts poetry's new media presence, turn on the television. In recent years poetry has become a code for sophistication. Sometimes entire poems are quoted. More often lines are quoted at critical junctures of the plot—sometimes with acknowledgment, sometimes without. Occasionally, a poem appears throughout an entire series as a thematic signal. *Breaking Bad* used Walt Whitman's "When I Heard the Learn'd Astronomer." *The Mentalist* employed William Blake's "The Tyger." Poetry is now even used in commercials. Volvo adapted Whitman's "Song of the Open Road." Apple iPad presented Robin Williams crooning the Good Gray Bard's "O Me! O Life!"

One might expect verse to appear in genteel hits such as *The Crown*, *Downton Abbey*, and *Victoria*. But poetry now works its way into such teen fare as *The Magicians*, *Supernatural*, *Legion*, *Fringe*, *Being Human*, *Penny Dreadful*, *Mr. Robot*, *Scream*, and *The Simpsons*. Poems are also frequently quoted on mainstream shows such as *Bones*, *Elementary*, *Forever*, *Revenge*, *Longmire*, *House of Cards*, *Castle*, *Mad Men*, *Parks and Recreation*, and *30 Rock*. It happens so often that the Netflix viewer is no longer surprised to hear Sheriff Longmire read John Donne in his Wyoming office or correct the scansion of a murderer's doggerel.

Poets now regularly appear as film and TV characters. This trend goes beyond literary biopics about Emily Dickinson, Sylvia Plath, Elizabeth Bishop, Pablo Neruda, and William Shakespeare. In the Netflix sci-fi series *Altered Carbon*, an Edgar Allan Poe replicant is the hero's sidekick. In *The Tudors*, Sir Thomas Wyatt and Earl of Surrey play major roles. Shakespeare pops up all over, most notably in his own flashy TNT series, *Will*, where not only Christopher Marlowe and Robert Southwell but even the obscure Robert Greene play significant parts.

There are many factors behind this trend, but at least two things seem obvious. First, the film community finds poetry creatively potent—as a cultural reference, sign of sophistication, or proof of artistic seriousness. Second, media's mass audience hears bits of poetry on a regular basis, whether it remembers them or not. If poetry's place in American culture is essentially paradoxical, one should savor the irony that poetry's rapid emergence as an element in TV scripts occurred at the same time that print media was cutting back on poetry reviews and the education system was shrinking poetry's place in its utilitarian "language arts" curriculum. As elite culture has less use for poetry, popular culture has embraced it.

American poetry is currently full of such contradictory trends.

That's one reason why the articles announcing poetry's demise are usually right and wrong at the same time. The grim facts they report may well be apocalyptic, but what they measure isn't what currently matters. So often commentators miss the big new thing happening next door. No one in an Ivy League English department would have predicted the current vogue of teen poetry and pop verse novels just as no one predicted the creation of hip-hop poetry or the renewal of rhyme and meter forty years ago. The trends did not originate in the English department. How could Kool Herc change world poetry without an MFA?

The university's role in poetry may be the most complicated paradox of all. For decades, the expansion of academic writing programs provided a home for poets, first as students and later as instructors. Academia gave thousands of poets secure, paid employment—something unprecedented in the history of Western literature. It was America's version of the Imperial Mandarin system, which once employed poets as bureaucrats across China's vast empire. Our system was even better. Poets got summers off.

Then, like most booms, the surge ended. The university system stopped expanding, especially in the humanities. Job applicants greatly outnumbered job openings. Rather than address the problem by cutting back graduate programs, universities chose to exploit their junior personnel as a cost savings. Tenure-track careers became adjunct gigs with low pay, no benefits, and minimal job security. The academic situation is old news, but it is still awful to the young and often not-so-young people caught up in crappy jobs or no jobs at all. The tale of this city clearly depends on what side of the tenure track a poet lives.

Academia's problems, however, had an unexpected cultural benefit. The legions of young writers, artists, musicians, and scholars who met with disappointment in the academic job market haven't all vanished. Most of them just moved. Not finding a place in one world, the academic refugees sought new lives in another. As old bohemian neighborhoods in Lower Manhattan, San Francisco, and other cities were being destroyed by gentrification, tourism, and rising real estate prices, a steady stream of unemployed and underemployed artists helped enlarge or create new communities in places like Oakland, Austin, Portland, Jersey City, Astoria, or downtown Los Angeles. Here they joined and revitalized preexisting local communities. Bohemian communities have also emerged in smaller towns, but in such cases their size makes them vulnerable to tourism and development. Witness the stultifying impact of money on Aspen and Carmel or on a larger scale the French Quarter of New Orleans and Santa Fe.

Thirty years ago the typical young poet taught in the university. Today's new generation is more likely to be living in a big city and employed outside academia. They work as baristas, brewers, and bookstore clerks; they also work in the law, medicine, and business. Technology has made it possible to publish books without institutional or commercial support. Social media connects people more effectively than any faculty lounge. An online journal requires nothing but time. A phone and a laptop can produce a professional poetry video. Any bookstore, library, café, or gallery can host a poetry reading.

New circumstances create interesting possibilities for poets. In the new bohemia a poet doesn't need to worry about tenure, peer review, or academic fashions. A poet doesn't even need a degree. Audience is not an abstract entity; the poet sees a diverse crowd at readings. Those faces are not the same ones found at a research university. The new communities include large parts of the population unlikely to participate in academic literary life because they are blocked by poverty, education, language, and race. Those groups have brought new perspectives and new energy to literary life. Minority authors and audiences often share a conviction that literature and literacy are fundamental to the identity, advancement, and even survival of their communities. When creating your own literature becomes a life or death issue, different sorts of poetry emerges than what one commonly finds in an English department.

The new bohemia is no demi-Eden. Writers struggle to balance their art with practical exigencies. Their situation is complicated but exciting. Existing outside both the academic and market economy makes these poets marginal in society, but their circumstances also give them freedom from commercial and academic conventions. Most boho writers, with or without degrees, probably still dream of snagging a professorship, but they also recognize that as outsider artists they represent an important cultural enterprise. Together they have created a vigorous alternative culture that has broken the university's monopoly on poetry. They have diversified, democratized, and localized American poetry.

The situation of poetry is impossible to describe but easy to summarize. No one fully understands what is happening because poetry and its audience are changing too quickly in too many places. There is considerable continuity with the past. The traditional ways in which poetry has been written, read, and evaluated still have relevance, but those methods don't always seem very useful in understanding new developments. Old theories (including postmodern ones) are incommensurate with the present realities. There is no emerging mainstream replacing a dying old order. There is no mainstream at all—only more alternatives. The best metaphor is not death but birth. The poetry scene isn't a cemetery; it's a crowded, noisy maternity ward.

So don't panic. Poetry is not in danger, at least no more than usual. New forms of poetry don't eliminate established forms. They do, however, influence and modify them. Culture is not binary but dialectical. Poetry now has as many competing categories and audience segments as popular music. What plays at Harvard won't get anyone on the dance floor in East Los Angeles, and that's just fine. All styles are possible, all approaches open, and everyone is invited.

★   ★   ★

When David Lehman asked me to edit the 2018 edition of *The Best American Poetry*, my first impulse was to decline. What an impossible task it would be to read and evaluate all the new poetry being published! Selecting the best poems of the year is made even more difficult because there is currently no consensus on what constitutes a poem, not to mention a "best" poem. For starters, how do you even define "poetry" when the term is used to describe a broad range of artistic forms from word art to hip-hop? Is poetry a graphic, typographic, audiovisual, or auditory medium? The answer is always yes. You or I may practice the art in a particular manner, but "poetry" now encompasses many different ways of compressing words into expressive shape. No wonder American poetics has become so contentious. My own taste in poetry is broad, but can any single editor have sympathies broad enough to evaluate everything fairly? Each volume of *The Best American Poetry* is necessarily an exercise in individual sensibility.

Why did I accept the offer? As A. E. Housman once remarked, vanity is the poet's ruling vice. It was an honor to join the celebrious ranks of previous editors. There was, however, another motivation—curiosity, that imp of the perverse who got Pandora into such trouble. I was curious about new poetry, especially the multitudinous work of the younger generation. Twenty-five years ago when I still made my living as a literary journalist, I had a better sense of new poetry. I reviewed books, read for prize committees, judged manuscripts for competitions, participated in writers' conferences, edited anthologies. I could, with difficulty, almost keep up. As I got older, the writers got younger and more numerous. The poetry world kept expanding, segmenting, and evolving. This project was my chance to catch up.

My editorial method was simple and entirely unoriginal. For twelve months (starting in October 2016) I spent two or three hours each day reading new poetry. I read through every journal I could find as well as dozens of online journals. I bought piles of unfamiliar small magazines and subscribed to new journals. I read every issue of every literary magazine in my university's large periodical room. When I traveled, I brought along a separate bag of journals to read on the plane or in the hotel room. Meanwhile the series editor sent me weekly packets of poems that had caught his attention. I initially wondered if David Lehman might want to press his suggestions. He is a persuasive advocate for the poetry he loves. Lehman, however, gave me complete editorial autonomy. I told no one outside my family that I had taken on the assignment. I didn't want to be lobbied by poet friends and acquaintances.

I'm not sure how many thousands of poems I read. I surely broke the five-digit mark. Every time a poem grabbed my attention, I earmarked it or printed it out for rereading. My studio became a mountain range of periodicals, printouts, and photocopies. The most interesting part of the process was rereading and comparing the hundreds of poems that had made the first cut. Week after week I read and sorted the poems into three scientific categories—Yes, No, Maybe. After much agonizing, I made the final selections.

Every editor has an agenda. I had two main goals. The first was to include the broadest variety of poems possible. American poetry is a wildly inclusive enterprise, full of innovations, continuities, contradictions, and idiosyncrasies. If one doesn't capture the diversity of style, theme, and perspective, the editor isn't doing a good job. I wanted long poems, short poems, lyrics, narratives, visions, satires, prayers, rants, protests, confessions, and collages. I wanted sonnets to sit next to prose poems, light verse to cohabit with elegies.

I did face one practical limit. The present volume focuses on forms of poetry that can be reproduced on the printed page in standard type. I would have liked to include some spoken poetry and hip-hop, but those auditory and performative modes lose impact when transcribed. To present them effectively would require electronic reproduction, which is beyond the scope of the book.

I also wanted to represent the social complexity of the country.

There may never have been so many races, cultures, religions, and lifestyles coexisting, conflicting, and often merging as in America today. That myriad of perspectives needed to be reflected. I also wanted to capture our poetry's regional variety. If *The Best American Poetry* doesn't have a national perspective, it isn't being true to its ambitious title. New York City remains the nation's literary capital, but it exercises no monopoly on poetic excellence. MFA programs have spread writers across the country. Strong regional centers, supported by powerful institutions such as the Library of Congress or the Poetry Foundation, have emerged in Chicago, Washington, San Francisco, Los Angeles, and Boston. There are fine writers everywhere.

My second goal was to include only poems that evoked a deep personal response. The sort of response might vary—wonder, delight, terror, fascination, gratitude. My taste is not perfect, but it is all I have to register the human effect of a poem. I see too many anthologies in which editors include the things that they are supposed to like. The books feel joyless and antiseptic. For me, the essence of poetry is an individual voice speaking to an individual reader. I didn't want to lose that subjectivity or intimacy. The poems in this book were chosen by a person, not by a committee.

If you spend a year of your finite life reading thousands of new poems, it is impossible to convey the thoughts and emotions you experience. The impact of this daily rhythm is too intense, frustrating, amazing, indulgent—too everything. Poems trigger emotions, ideas, and memories. You notice strange things. You change your opinions. You get great flashes of insight that you can't remember the next morning. To describe the process would require a book-length journal, but that book would be more about the reader than the poems. Instead, I made notes about the poems. Here are a few basic things I noticed—not just about the poems in the book but the larger body of new work I read.

First, a few words about style because the news is so positive. We have now decisively entered the Cole Porter period of American poetry—anything goes. The poetry wars of the late twentieth century have been forgotten. Form and free verse are no longer viewed as mutually exclusive techniques. A benevolent sanity prevails in which poets seem free to write in whatever way inspiration suggests. I was pleased to see individual writers publish work in widely different styles, sometimes even in the same issue of a journal. Free verse remains the dominant mode, but rhyme and meter are widely used again, often in ways that imitate hip-hop. Prose poems still make a strong showing. The haiku tradition continues to thrive, though mostly in its own subculture. My biggest surprise was the surge in sonnets. I had not expected to find so many, often in such unlikely places and written by poets not usually associated with form. It was a pleasure to turn the pages of a journal and not know what to expect next.

I was interested in what poets wrote about. Had the themes and subjects changed much in recent years? It wasn't always what I expected. American poetry remains very autobiographical—no surprise there. The most common subject in the thousands of poems I read was "Family." Today's poets still deeply identify themselves with their personal origins, whether those domestic sources were happy or sad.

The next most common subject was also autobiographical—"Childhood and Adolescence," which, of course, overlaps with "Family." Then came "Love," which often took the form of describing early sexual experience with its manifold discoveries and disappointments. Then came my big surprise. The fourth most common topic was "Poetry." I couldn't believe how many poems I read about poetry, poets, teaching poetry, or being a poet. I suspect that the subject's ubiquity came from equal parts of anxiety and fascination. Defining what it means to be a poet in a society that doesn't give poets an established place clearly preoccupies American writers. Poets feel a need to explore and articulate their artistic identities.

The top five themes were rounded out—naturally—by "Nature," though it might be more accurate to say "Nature and the Environment." I had expected to see more political poetry. (There was, of course, a time lag in effect: most of the poems I read had been written before the last presidential election.) I realized, however, that the nature poem had become the major vehicle for political meditation and protest. The bright innocence of Walt Whitman's American Eden has been overtaken by Robinson Jeffers's dark prophesy of rapacious modern civilization. The natural world is no longer a secure source of joy and renewal for poets; it is a matrix of anxiety about human despoliation and ecological apocalypse. The text may be nature, but the subtext is environmental disaster.

If nature poetry has become a medium for public politics, then Family, Childhood, Love, and Poetry were also often vehicles to explore the politics of personal identity. In a nation where individual writers no longer feel confident they will be heard, personal politics has overtaken civic politics as the main mode of protest poetry. To assert the right to one's own voice and values has become a form of dissent. What better medium than poetry to insist on the voice of the individual?

Those were a few things I noticed. I probably missed the biggest trend. How do you measure something that won't hold still? American poetry is now so large, complex, and dynamic that no one can accurately describe it. At least I can't. I gave it my best for twelve months. Now my job is to get out of the way, and let seventy-five other poets do the talking.

THE
BEST
AMERICAN
POETRY
2018

Miscarriage

◊   ◊   ◊

The colors are off. Muted, like a confession.
That's what drew me to it, this rug
in the middle of my living
room floor. I found it enchanting.

We'd lost our first
to moths—what could we do?
It was their season.
I didn't know how to save things.

This one would be different.
Woven into the pattern were women
facing one another, each passing
a small, blurry object to the next. I was

determined to take better care this time—
swept and scrubbed, tried
to comb out of the fibers anything wrong, unnatural.
The wood planks bowed as I worked.

But something had already laid its eggs
in a place I couldn't reach.
The women in the carpet looked away
as if they knew what they'd come to deliver.

from *Southwest Review*

Against Dying

◊   ◊   ◊

if the body is just a parable
about the body if breath
is a leash to hold the mind
then staying alive should be
easier than it is most sick
things become dead things
at twenty-four my liver was
already covered in fatty
rot my mother filled a tiny
coffin with picture frames
I spent the year drinking
from test tubes weeping
wherever I went somehow
it happened wellness crept
into me like a roach nibbling
through an eardrum for
a time the half-minutes
of fire in my brainstem
made me want to pull out
my spine but even those
have become bearable so
how shall I live now
in the unexpected present
I spent so long in a lover's
quarrel with my flesh
the peace seems over-
cautious too-polite I say
stop being cold or *make
that blue bluer* and it does

we speak to each other
in this code where every word
means *obey* I sit under
a poplar tree with a thermos
of chamomile feeling
useless as an oath against
dying I put a sugar cube
on my tongue and
swallow it like a pill

from *Tin House*

JULIA ALVAREZ

American Dreams

◇   ◇   ◇

Queens, NY, 1963

All day I dreamed of candy from the store
on Hillside Avenue: barrels filled with
caramels, tins of pastel mints and tiers
of chocolates beckoning in the window,
and a tinkling bell that tattled I was coming
in the door, a skinny girl, who didn't look
thirteen, still reeling from the shock of
losing everything, and hungry all the time
for candy, more candy than I'd ever seen,
a whole store dedicated to delights,
proof we had arrived in the land of Milk
Duds, Chiclets, gumdrops, from the country
sugar came from but candy never got to.
I roamed the aisles, savoring the names:
Necco Wafers, Atomic Fireballs, Butterfingers,
while the fat man owner watched me, sitting
on a stool by the cash register; his pale eyes
like ice mints behind his foggy glasses, lingering
at my chest, as if the swelling buds under
my uniform's white blouse were Candy Buttons,
Jujubes I'd shoplifted; while his tiny, perfumed
mother in black pumps and white lace collar
waited on older patrons, boxing chocolates,
petit-fours, assortments made to order
for wives and sweethearts, *May I help you, dahlink?*
in a heavy accent, an immigrant herself
from some past purge or pogrom; her "boy"

4

born here, the obese product of an American
dream gone greedily awry. He chatted as I
lingered over barrels, asking none-of-your-
business questions about my parents, grades,
what my people did on holidays. He knew
my favorites, commenting as he rang me up,
*I see you like those SweeTarts. Candy Necklaces
sure are a hit with your set.* A hit? My set?
It was an intimacy I resented; my cravings
were dark secrets I didn't want to share.
Will that be all today? he asked, as if he hoped
I'd say, *Actually, I would like something else,
to marry you and help you run your candy store.*
Outside, my new America was waking up
to nightmare: freedom fighters
marching; storefronts, some with candy
stores like this one, burning; girls like me
in bombed-out churches; dreams deferred,
exploding; dreams I didn't know
still needed fighting for; all I knew
was hunger, as I learned the names
that promised sweeter dreams beyond
these candied substitutes, Juicy Fruits,
Life Savers, Bit-O-Honey, Good & Plenty.

from *America*

A . R . A M M O N S

Finishing Up

◊   ◊   ◊

I wonder if I know enough to know what it's really like
to have been here: have I seen sights enough to give
seeing over: the clouds, I've waited with white
October clouds like these this afternoon often before and

taken them in, but white clouds shade other white
ones gray, had I noticed that: and though I've
followed the leaves of many falls, have I spent time with
the wire vines left when frost's red dyes strip the leaves

away: is more missing than was never enough: I'm sure
many of love's kinds absolve and heal, but were they passing
rapids or welling stirs: I suppose I haven't done and seen
enough yet to go, and, anyway, it may be way on on the way

before one picks up the track of the sufficient, the
world-round reach, spirit deep, easing and all, not just mind
answering itself but mind and things apprehended at once
as one, all giving all way, not a scrap of question holding back.

from *Poetry*

Sherpa Song

◊   ◊   ◊

Your rope, my rope. My tracks,
Your steps. Beneath my feet,
The drop. Around my waist.
Your weight. On my back,
Your stuff, my yoke, the works.

Your pace, my pace. My task,
Your quest. Underfoot, crack
After crack, the ice, the ice.
Above and beyond, our route,
The world's roof, a roost of mist.

Over one shoulder, a yelp
Downslope, a whoop back up:
My jabber, your babble, our heart
To heart in the heat of our assault
On the last face, pitch by pitch.

Up top, tapped out: your breath,
My breath, gasp for gasp, our
Dragon clouds. Out there, nowhere
But here, where air comes dear:
No far, no near, the end of all roads.

Your neck, my neck. Your cross,
My wind horse. Your mule,
My ass: try soulmate, your muse,
My own man. Under my mask,
My real mask, your open book.

from *Southwest Review*

ANDREW BERTAINA

A Translator's Note

◇   ◇   ◇

The translation, admittedly, has a number of defects, which are at least partially attributable to the fact that I cannot read Italian. And yet I have tried when possible to capture the pure essence of what the esteemed writer's language probably meant. In certain passages, I'd humbly argue that my translation surpasses those of all three prior translations of the author's work. Those translators had at their disposal only a working knowledge of Italian and small academic grants that allowed them to spend countless hours in dim libraries, parsing his words and trying to account for all nuances of meaning before settling on the correct word. While I, being slightly older than all three, have the great and unattainable thing of which they can only dream.

I saw the great writer once at a book shop in Venice. It was near the end of his life and the skin sagged from his face like cloth from a sail. He was across the room from me, behind old leather-bound volumes, and a globe which showed an outsized version of Italy. His great white beard and unkempt hair, falling to near his shoulders, made him immediately identifiable. He was, this great man, leaning in very close to hear the words of a very beautiful woman, but I could see the twinkle in his eye, the soul not yet at rest. From that moment, I have gathered all of my inspiration for the text, and though it may differ occasionally in form, content, and certain items of the plot, I confess to you, reader, that no one knew him better than I and that I can confidently declare this work the definitive translation.

from *The Threepenny Review*

Mourning What We Thought We Were

◇   ◇   ◇

We were born into an amazing experiment.
At least we thought we were. We knew there was no
escaping human nature: my grandmother

taught me that: my own pitiless nature
taught me that: but we exist inside an order, I

thought, of which history
is the mere shadow—

★

Every serious work of art about America has the same
theme: *America*

is a great Idea: the reality leaves something to be desired.

Bakersfield. Marian Anderson, the first great black classical
contralto, whom the Daughters of the American Revolution

would not allow to sing in an unsegregated

Constitution Hall, who then was asked by Eleanor
Roosevelt to sing at the Lincoln Memorial before thousands

was refused a room at the Padre Hotel, Bakersfield.

My mother's disgust
as she told me this. It confirmed her judgment about

what she never could escape, where she lived out her life.

My grandmother's fury when, at the age of seven or
eight, I had eaten at the home of a black friend.

The forced camps at the end of *The Grapes of Wrath*
were outside

Bakersfield. When I was a kid, *Okie*

was still a common term of casual derision and contempt.

★

So it was up to us, born
in Bakersfield, to carve a new history

of which history is the mere shadow—

★

To further the history of the spirit is our work:

therefore thank you, Lord
Whose Bounty Proceeds by Paradox,

for showing us we have failed to change.

★

Dark night, December 1st 2016.

White supremacists, once again in
America, are acceptable, respectable. America!

Bakersfield was first swamp, then
desert. We are sons of the desert
who cultivate the top half-inch of soil.

from *The New Yorker*

Anthem

◊   ◊   ◊

The music of the anthem has no boundary,
no sworn allegiance, no nation save
the one we lower into its dying body.
A soldier kneels over a soldier's grave,
and the tune is not the name he reads
but the hand that brushes the dirt to read it.
If you search the anthems of the world,
you see grief turn to pride, pride to spite.
Soon a motherland is deaf with words.
The music of the anthem does not decry
the politics of dissonance or closure.
It affirms nothing. And thus, it never lies,
never breaks the news in secret, the sons
set down in steady heartbeats: one, one, one.

from *Denver Quarterly*

Those Were the Days

◇   ◇   ◇

We were happy as pigs in whatever makes a pig happy.
We caught world-class nightcrawlers in the rise-and-shine, and the pinguid
      poultry was as much as we could handle.
Seamstresses back then were many and available and kept us in stitches any time.
It was all good as gold, whether it glittered or not.

We averted our eyes before we leapt, and we landed on our own two knees.
We took misunderstandings right out of each other's mouth.
Sure, we had needy acquaintances: some things don't change.
Our money insisted on a trial separation, and you'd feel foolish, too.

We proposed nonstop, but God was mostly indisposed.
We called all cookware colorless, to be on the safe side.
Clothes made the men and unmade the women, so everybody opted for T-shirts
      and cargo pants, and we grew to fit the container.
We used it up, we wore it out, we made it do, as do the trout.

A penny saved was half a cent.
We guzzled wine for auld lang syne and said the buzz was never better.
We lost the drum and kept on marching.
As a rule we were safe. In the end we were sorry anyway.

from *Raritan*

Birds Punctuate the Days

◇   ◇   ◇

apostrophe
the nuthatch inserts itself
between feeder and pole

semicolon
two mallards drifting
one dunks for a snail

ellipses
a mourning dove
lifts off

asterisk
a red-eyed vireo catches
the crane fly midair

comma
a down feather
bobs between waves

exclamation point
wren on the railing
takes notice

colon
mergansers paddle toward
morning trout swirl

em dash
at dusk a wild goose
heading east

question mark
the length of silence
after a loon's call

period
one blue egg all summer long
now gone

from *Modern Haiku*

The Opposites Game

◇   ◇   ◇

for Patricia Maisch

This day my students and I play the Opposites Game
with a line from Emily Dickinson. *My life had stood—
a loaded gun*, it goes and I write it on the board,
pausing so they can call out the antonyms—

My	Your
Life	Death
Had stood?	Will sit
A	Many
Loaded	Empty
Gun?	

Gun.
For a moment, very much like the one between
lightning and its sound, the children just stare at me,
and then it comes, a flurry, a hail storm of answers—

Flower, says one. No, Book, says another. That's stupid,
cries a third, the opposite of a gun is a pillow. Or maybe
a hug, but not a book, no way is it a book. With this,
the others gather their thoughts

and suddenly it's a shouting match. No one can agree,
for every student there's a final answer. It's a song,
a prayer, I mean a promise, like a wedding ring, and
later a baby. Or what's that person who delivers babies?

A midwife? Yes, a midwife. No, that's wrong. You're so
wrong you'll never be right again. It's a whisper, a star,
it's saying I love you into your hand and then touching
someone's ear. Are you crazy? Are you the president

of Stupid-land? You should be, When's the election?
It's a teddy bear, a sword, a perfect, perfect peach.
Go back to the first one, it's a flower, a white rose.
When the bell rings, I reach for an eraser but a girl

snatches it from my hand. Nothing's decided, she says,
We're not done here. I leave all the answers
on the board. The next day some of them have
stopped talking to each other, they've taken sides.

There's a Flower club. And a Kitten club. And two boys
calling themselves The Snowballs. The rest have stuck
with the original game, which was to try to write
something like poetry.

It's a diamond, it's a dance,
the opposite of a gun is a museum in France.
It's the moon, it's a mirror,
it's the sound of a bell and the hearer.

The arguing starts again, more shouting, and finally
a new club. For the first time I dare to push them.
Maybe all of you are right, I say.

Well, maybe. Maybe it's everything we said. Maybe it's
everything we didn't say. It's words and the spaces for words.
They're looking at each other now. It's everything in this room
and outside this room and down the street and in the sky.

It's everyone on campus and at the mall, and all the people
waiting at the hospital. And at the post office. And, yeah,
it's a flower, too. All the flowers. The whole garden.
The opposite of a gun is wherever you point it.

Don't write that on the board, they say. Just say poem.
Your death will sit through many empty poems.

from *The American Journal of Poetry*

Prayer Concerning the New, More "Accurate" Translation of Certain Prayers

◊   ◊   ◊

O Lord of the inverted verb,
You Who alone *vouchsafe* and *deign*,
Whom simpler diction might perturb,
To Whom we may not make things plain,
Forgive us now this Job-like rant:
These prayers translated plumb-and-squarely
Pinch and constrict us (though we grant
They broaden our vocabulary).
Hear us still if we mutter dully
With uninflected tongues and knees,
Shunning (see Matthew 6) the poly-
Syllables of the Pharisees.
This we entreat, implore, beseech
Whose miseries are too deep for speech.

from *Rattle*

Toast to My Dead Parents

◇   ◇   ◇

My parents worshipped at the altar
of the present, each moment
an opportunity for bickering,
for one of them, in their elaborate game
of cat-and-mouse—*Didn't you say
it was going to rain today?
Who put the salt and pepper here,
it's gone in the cabinet above the stove
for sixty years*—to gain a slight advantage.

They were entertaining, their fights
like tickets to the Amusement Park
we could never afford.
My father, who liked wordplay,
said they were keeping things *fresh*.
They said good morning
in myriad phrases—*the eggs are dry,
you burnt the English muffin again,
where did you put my pills?*
That got the morning going like the cuckoo
popping out of the Black Forest
kitchen clock to jeeringly announce
the hour that was an hour too late,
each blaming the other for oversleeping.

It was, I guess, in its sad, crazy
destructive way, a form of communication.
My brothers and I never understood
their day-long bickering, nor that
nagging devotion to each other,
one of them unfailingly present
at the other's bedside in sickness.
They never complained about money,
lived happily by the house rule of *enough*,
as in whatever we have is enough,
yet seemed always to be in need
of something that wasn't to be had—
something intangible they wanted
to hold with their hands, or be
able to say with the fluency of words
which never came, or came
garbled and incompletely, or twisted
whatever they were looking for
into another insult.

Their bickering grew less playful,
more cat batting a half-dead mouse
back and forth between its paws,
as they tried to ward off
the clock-tick of dying's boredom.
They certainly kept things *fresh*,
the freedom of destruction, I guess,
better than some quiet descent
into death. And so, dear parents, I toast you,
toast all those words volleyed back and forth,
the two of you filled with some great need
that could never be fully met,
true believers in all that might be
that never was, hopeless
romantics to the bitter end.

from *The Sewanee Review*

Artaud

◊   ◊   ◊

At age five, with his sister Marie-Ange.

Around 1920 at age twenty-four.

Around 1920 at his sister's wedding.

As Cecco, in Marcel Vandal's film *Graziella* (1926).

As Gringalet, in Luitz-Morat's film *Le Juif errant* (1926).

As Marat, in Abel Gance's *Napoléon* (1927).

As Marat.

As the Intellectual, in Léon Poirier's film *Verdun, visions d'histoire* (1928).

As the monk Massieu, in Carl Dreyer's *La Passion de Jeanne d'Arc* (1928).

As the father in his play, *Les Cenci*, produced in 1935 by the Theater of Cruelty.

On the grounds of the asylum in Rodez, with Dr. Ferdière in May 1946.

Self-portrait (December 17, 1946).

His room in the clinic in Ivry-sur-Seine.

In his room, shortly before his death.

from *Bennington Review*

DICK DAVIS

A Personal Sonnet

◇   ◇   ◇

How strange this life is mine, and not another,
This jigsaw . . . each irrevocable piece.
That bad, unfinished business of my brother,
Dead at nineteen; my gadding years in Greece
And Italy; life lived, not understood;
A sunset in Kerala, when it seemed
The sun had risen on my life for good.
All this was real, but seems now as if dreamed.

The presences I've loved, and poetry—
Faces I cannot parse or paraphrase
Whose mystery is all that they reveal;
The Persian poets who laid hands on me
And whispered that all poetry is praise:
These are the dreams that turned out to be real.

from *The Hudson Review*

Today's Special

◊   ◊   ◊

Today's special is all-natural rage,
Grilled on a smoldering fire.
Its powerful flavor made subtle with age,
Today's special is all-natural rage.
Domestically raised in a comfortable cage,
And fed only free-range desire,
Today's special is all-natural rage,
Grilled on a smoldering fire.

from *Think Journal*

SUSAN DE SOLA

The Wives of the Poets

◊   ◊   ◊

> All poets' wives have rotten lives,
> Their husbands look at them like knives
> —*Delmore Schwartz*

The wives of the poets,
they never complain.
They know they are married
to drama and pain.

They know they are married
to more than their man.
They know there are others—
young lovers he can

fend off from the marriage
that keeps him afloat,
for rail as they may,
he won't rock that boat.

She won't read the poems
he's written for her;
the poems for lovers
will cause no great stir.

He knows she won't read them,
because her concern
is life (and not words)
but both feel the burn

of the daggers they throw,
the sharp looks that show
the rot in the lives
of poets, and wives.

from *The Dark Horse*

Reading Dostoyevsky at Seventeen

◊ ◊ ◊

In those days, my dreams always changed titles
before they were finished and I wanted
only to love in that insane tortured way
of poor dear Dmitri Karamazov.
Suddenly, I was speaking the language
of lapdog and samovar. This is
the ballroom, the barracks, the firing squad.
This is the old monk with the beard of bees.
This is the orange lullaby the moon
of the moon will sing you when it's grieving.
This is the province you escape by train,
fleeing heavy snow and eternal elk.
This is the part where I take your hand in
my hand and I tell you we are burning.

from *Met Magazine*

NAUSHEEN EUSUF

Pied Beauty

◊   ◊   ◊

Is it not the beauty of the maculate?
    The speckled, spotted, the rose now varicose;
    the sky now gold and now a purple bruise;
the taint and sully of the soul's caprice;
    the fitful orisons of a restless hour;
    the artful heart so fickle-quick to sour.

Whatever wavers with the changing minute:
the weather, the markets, the 401 and peace
    of mind; what had been promised but never meant;
    the youth and years that now seem badly spent—

Accept it.

from *Birmingham Poetry Review*

JONATHAN GALASSI

Orient Epithalamion

◊   ◊   ◊

for Barry Bergdoll and Bill Ryall

Fall will touch down in golden Orient,
where ospreys float and peace comes dropping slow.
There will be pumpkins by the ton at Latham's.
The trees will re-rehearse their yearly show.

But now crepe myrtle ornaments the village,
rose of Sharon, autumn clematis.
The oyster ponds are dark and tranquil mirrors
basking in the sunlight's brazen kiss.

On Skipper's Lane, Sebastian and Sarah
have packed up with their brood, as one expects,
and Madeline and Chris, and Jane and Eddie.
No more artists! No more architects!

Just Miriam and Grayson, Sylvia and Freddie.
Gone: writers, agents, publishers, and all!
The real people, proudly holding steady,
will reap the blond munificence of fall.

Goodbye to the disturbances of summer,
when Stevie's singers jazzed in Poquatuck
and a Supreme Court Justice read our rights out
to every citizen, man, doe, and buck.

Now egrets dot the marsh on Narrow River.
The swan is hiding till she nests next spring.

Virginia creeper reddens on the tree trunks.
Goldenrod envelops everything,

succeeding to swamp rose and honeysuckle
and all the weeds that came and went in waves.
The geese will soon be flying in formation
the way the Tuthill slaves sleep in their graves.

Near the monarch station, the Holzapfels
harvest their garlic. Milkweed is in flower.
Leslie's pool is cooling down. The ferry
disgorges only fifty cars an hour.

It's time for sweet bay scallops, now the jellies
have turned tail in the Sound and sped away.
The Bogdens lay their conch pots every morning,
and the water climbs in Hallock's Bay.

Charles the First is staking lilies. Sinan
reduces his last oozings, hours by hours.
Karen surveys the still street from her study.
Charles the Second's arms are full of flowers.

And the wild turkeys make their first appearance,
though Bay and Sound still glisten from the Hill.
The vineyard grapes hang blithe and ripe and ruddy.
Ann builds her house and Barry marries Bill.

Wreathe them with sea lavender and asters!
Sing for the joys and years they have in store.
Husband them; preserve them from disasters.
Let there be jazzing in the deep heart's core—

and let the tide not overrun the causeway:
may Orient be theirs forever more!

from *The New Yorker*

Test

◇   ◇   ◇

Mrs. Yeager's handout of college prep vocab words
was meant as an *onerous* task for a *neophyte*, a *germane lexicon*,
but I *ascertained* first what had been my uncle's initials: S A T.
I heard no more of the lecture, repeated silently his *moniker*.
Was this (a) *auspicious*; (b) *ominous*; (c) merely *benign*?

My mother's only story: how my uncle, between all-
night shifts at the post office and *arduous* college courses,
used to rouse and feed an infant me, his hand to my mouth.
Otherwise she kept a silence in which I learned *ambiguous*,
lugubrious, and *truncate*. Through my uncle's absence
I memorized *doleful*, *evanescent*, and *curtailed* by heart.

"Choose the best answer from the following." The sentence suggests
there *is* a best answer for an empty mouth. Mortality is
(a) *conditional*; (b) *congenital*; (c) *incompatible*; (d) *superfluous*.
Death is (a) *insatiable*; (b) *inexorable*; (c) *ineffable*; (d) *immutable*.
I am (a) the niece of no body; (b) death's little *dilettante*;
(c) *consanguine* with hoar frost; (d) kin to white noise.

from *The Southern Review*

Ghost Ship

◇   ◇   ◇

I have been that young, that electrified
by the bohemian scene of a city spilling its lights
all around me. I have been to parties
in sketchy spaces where painters have work
on the walls that should be seen by millions
but is seen by the few of us figuring out
who we're going to fuck after too much cheap wine
drunk from plastic tumblers, figuring out
how we're going to make it a country's width away
from families, struck out on our own
like explorers getting comfortable with being alone
in a wilderness that is actually just a room
rented in a house of strangers. I have been
that woman high on E, my eyes doll-dark, jaw
clenched, body ready to swallow pleasure
in a million lusty gulps. I know any space we inhabit
can become a ghost ship. I have read enough
to know stories of wildfires, of boats found
empty, of the soul yanked whole cloth from
its innocent wearer. But you can't live in fear
of the apparition, the adventurers afloat on
their rickety structure and cast to a sea
of flames. It can happen at any time to anyone,
so when music flares up and takes a hold of you,
when a swirl of colored spotlights sets you
spinning, you have to dance as if
the very act of living depends on it.

from *Rattle*

An American Sunrise

◇   ◇   ◇

We were running out of breath, as we ran out to meet ourselves. We
were surfacing the edge of our ancestors' fights, and ready to strike.
It was difficult to lose days in the Indian bar if you were straight.
Easy if you played pool and drank to remember to forget. We
made plans to be professional—and did. And some of us could sing
so we drummed a fire-lit pathway up to those starry stars. Sin
was invented by the Christians, as was the Devil, we sang. We
were the heathens, but needed to be saved from them—thin
chance. We knew we were all related in this story, a little gin
will clarify the dark and make us all feel like dancing. We
had something to do with the origins of blues and jazz
I argued with the music as I filled the jukebox with dimes in June.

Forty years later and we still want justice. We are still America. We
know the rumors of our demise. We spit them out. They die soon.

from *Poetry*

American Sonnet for My Past and Future Assassin

◊   ◊   ◊

The black poet would love to say his century began
With Hughes or, God forbid, Wheatley, but actually
It began with all the poetry weirdos & worriers, warriors,
Poetry whiners & winos falling from ship bows, sunset
Bridges & windows. In a second I'll tell you how little
Writing rescues. My hunch is that Sylvia Plath was not
Especially fun company. A drama queen, thin-skinned,
And skittery, she thought her poems were ordinary.
What do you call a visionary who does not recognize
Her vision? Orpheus was alone when he invented writing.
His manic drawing became a kind of writing when he sent
His beloved a sketch of an eye with an X struck through it.
He meant *I am blind without you*. She thought he meant
I never want to see you again. It is possible he meant that, too.

from *The New Yorker*

ERNEST HILBERT

Mars Ultor

◊   ◊   ◊

Before they had a fleet
Romans rowed on logs
As they prepared to meet

Carthage. Treaties, public
Or secret, do little when
The border of the republic

Is breached without notice:
More tug-of-war
Than elegant chess.

Some ask: Is *virtù* virtue?
After reconciliation, consensus,
Appeasement, the coup.

Some rely on law,
But law relies on guns,
Or must withdraw.

Brutes push their way to power,
But the muddiest barbarian
Also wants the throne an hour,

And dons a crown, marks affairs,
Nods under a golden branch until
A stronger one turns up the stairs.

from *Academic Questions*

The View from The Bar

◊   ◊   ◊

So much of the coin of youth was spent,
while leaning here, with smoke and brew,

my back half-turned to face a view
beyond this room's brief consequence.

So many nights washed up against
my eyes in their impassive mask

and touched this quadrangle of glass,
this lens where all the sediments

of moving traffic sink at last
to a surface whose impermanence

holds translucent evidence
of what has come, again, to pass.

Before me—this screen of calm abstraction,
a frieze of captured light on glass.

Behind me—bodies, weight and mass,
rehearsing lanes of interaction,

drinking their sloe-gins and rums,
picking daisies, snorting roses,

practicing Pompeian poses—
at least until the lava comes.

For when it comes, we'll *all* be frozen,
some on the dance floor, some in the street,

one in his usual window seat,
each in a pose he's not quite chosen.

(New York City—1995)

from *The Hopkins Review*

TONY HOAGLAND

Into the Mystery

◊　◊　◊

Of course there is a time of afternoon, out there in the yard,
a time that has never been described.

There is the way the air feels
among the flagstones and the tropical plants
                    with their dark, leathery-green leaves.

There is a gap you never noticed,
dug out between the gravel and the rock, where something lives.

There is a bird that can only be heard by someone
who has come to be alone.

Now you are getting used to things that will not be happening again.

Never to be pushed down onto the bed again, laughing,
and have your clothes unbuttoned.

Never to stand up in the rear of the pickup truck
and scream, while blasting out of town.

This life that rushes over everything,
like water or like wind, and wears it down until it shines.

Now you sit on the brick wall in the cloudy afternoon, and swing
                    your legs,
happy because there never has been a word for this

as you continue moving through these days and years
where more and more the message is

                              not to measure anything.

            from *The Sun*

ANNA MARIA HONG

Yonder, a Rental

◇   ◇   ◇

Time to howl at the celestial sphere,
that full frontal silver dollar, the very
paintball of pallor and elemental other.
It's all or nada as noon-night's empanada

discloses her pretty quarter, the priest's collar
hung high on the hook of evening's fluent
wall. Hung like a juror bent on acquittal
who can't stall any longer, you're a cobbler

hawking copper coins in an Oriental
bazaar. The Sultan's power went horizontal
long, long ago. It's fine to be sentimental,

though there's no need to bother. Grab a handful
of shine like a disc of doll hair, a dollop
of Neufchâtel,
                      valor and force, vital—

from *Ecotone*

"I Am the Size of What I See"

◊   ◊   ◊

—*Fernando Pessoa*

You hurry but you are late
to every party and dinner date,
so naturally they begin without you.
Like a pale leaf through the window,
you make your entrance secretly.
Now you can shine in the corner
as quietly as any leaf,
rarely speaking and then in puzzles;
in English when they are Spanish,
in cliff-edge when they are hanging.
They are the size of what they see,
swimming in their vocabularies
of desire and principal interest.

You're a bird too young to fly,
a map without its pink and salmon.
You're so late you arrive on time,
and later slip out unnoticed,
not even a smudge on your glass.
They never knew what passed them.

You walk to the absolute corner,
where the roof of the sky
meets the limit of the eye
and a breath lasts a lifetime.

Beautiful dreamer,
you're the size of what you see.
The sky is the size of the sky,
and the sun is just the sun.
But a tree is the size of the flame
you hold in your fingers.

What shirt to wear to eternity
and tomorrow to dinner?
And what size will it be?
You're asking while you can.
There are things you can't forget
like the life before this one.

from *Fifth Wednesday Journal*

MARIE HOWE

Walking Home

◇   ◇   ◇

Everything dies, I said. How had that started?
A tree? The winter? Not me, she said.

And I said, Oh yeah? And she said, I'm reincarnating.
Ha, she said, See you in a few thousand years!

Why years, I wondered, why not minutes? Days?
She found that so funny—Ha Ha—doubled over—

Years, she said, confidently.
I think you and I have known each other a few lifetimes, I said.

She said, I have never before been a soul on this earth.
(It was cold. We were hungry.) Next time, you be the mother, I said.

No way, Jose, she said, as we turned the last windy corner.

from *The New York Times Magazine*

Ives

◇   ◇   ◇

Oh to be Charles Ives, who wrote for the future
and lived in an organized present,
who filed away each symphony
in a leather sleeve and took the train
from a garden house in Connecticut
to a seat at a corporate desk. Think of Mozart,
wild with sorrow, dodging debtors, out of work,
and Ives is on his train ride watching trees arrange their boughs.
He hasn't had a concert in twenty years,
and there he is, beating out dissonant lines
on his two pressed lapels.
He's not the cat that ate the bright canary
but the cat who holds the bright canary live
inside the mouth. He's the cat that feels it breathing,
the cat that will not speak or smile,
the cat that godly patience fills with peace.

from *Ambit*

ILYA KAMINSKY

We Lived Happily During the War

◊ ◊ ◊

And when they bombed other people's houses, we

protested
but not enough, we opposed them but not

enough. I was
in my bed, around my bed America

was falling: invisible house by invisible house by invisible house.

I took a chair outside and watched the sun.

       In the sixth month
of a disastrous reign in the house of money

in the street of money in the city of money in the country of money,
our great country of money, we (forgive us)

lived happily during the war.

from *The American Poetry Review*

The Quiet Boy

◊   ◊   ◊

The talk turned, as it always did, to power,
Or more precisely, to the superpowers
The boys would die for. All of them were boys.

They camped out in the corner of the band room
During lunch hours that felt too long for them,
Extracting chips and Cheetos from their bags

While they discussed telepathy, time travel,
Teleportation, and the finer points
Of flight: "Of course it's badass," said the one

Who said most everything as if he knew
Most everything, "but you can go too high,
And then what?" Here he hammed it up: gasps, gurgles.

"Can't breathe. You pass out. Then you better hope
You turn invincible before you land."
He crunched his Bugle with authority.

"Pyrokinesis," purred the lone bold boy
Who dared to smoke. "Oh, please," another countered,
"Hydrokinesis. Since we're mostly water."

"Invisibility," daydreamed the boy
With acne so persistent and intense—
His face pink, amber-grainy, strafed with strips

Of peeling skin—he seemed a poorly made
Piñata, "I'd pick that one. Just imagine
The things you'd see!" The boys all paused then, lost

In puffs and pallors none of them had seen
Except online. One wiped his salty fingers
Across his jeans. Another gulped his Crush.

The quiet boy, as usual, said nothing.
Invisibility? Dumb. Just plain dumb.
Why choose a power you already had?

from *Birmingham Poetry Review*

DONIKA KELLY

Love Poem: Chimera

◇   ◇   ◇

I thought myself lion and serpent. Thought
myself body enough for two, for we.
Found comfort in never being lonely.

What burst from my back, from my bones, what lived
along the ridge from crown to crown, from mane
to forked tongue beneath the skin. What clamor

we made in the birthing. What hiss and rumble
at the splitting, at the horns and beard,
at the glottal bleat. What bridges our back.

What strong neck, what bright eye. What menagerie
are we. What we've made of ourselves.

from *Gulf Coast*

Sono

◇   ◇   ◇

Out of albumen and blood, out of amniotic brine,
placental sea-swell, trough, salt-spume and foam,

you came to us infinitely far, little traveler, from the other world—
skull-keel and heel-hull socketed to pelvic cradle,

rib-rigging, bowsprit-spine, driftwood-bone,
the ship of you scudding wave after wave of what-might-never-have-been.

Memory, stay faithful to this moment, which will never return:
may I never forget when we first saw you, there on the other side,

still fish-gilled, water-lunged,
your eelgrass-hair and seahorse-skeleton floating in the sonogram screen

like a ghost from tomorrow,
moth-breath quicksilver in snowy pixels, fists in sleep-twitch,

not yet alive but not *not*,
you who were and were not,

a thunder of bloodbeats sutured in green jags on the ultrasound machine
like hooves galloping from eternity to time,

feet kicking bone-creel and womb-wall,
while we waited, never to waken in that world again,

the world without the shadow of your death,
with no you or not-you, no *is* or *was* or *might-have-been* or *never-were*.

May I never forget when we first saw you in your afterlife
which was life,

soaked otter-pelt and swan-down crowning,
face cauled in blood and mucus-mud, eyes soldered shut,

wet birth-cord rooting you from one world to the next,
you who might not have lived, might never have been born, like all the others,

as we looked at every pock and crook of your skull,
every clotted hair, seal-slick on your blue-black scalp,

every lash, every nail, every pore, every breath,
with so much wonder that wonder is not the word—

from *Southword*

Palazzo Maldura

◇   ◇   ◇

The palazzo library was a retrofit,
    and as usual I was book-worming
    through the metal stacks that morning,
the photocopier in the corner on its time out

where the frescoes had started to spall,
    nymphs and satyrs scuffed by human traffic
    as they danced to a sensual music.
But I ignored their pipe and timbrel,

intent on some offprint or quarto.
    In the beginning you do not know yourself,
    and then there follow years of
knowing only what you do not know,

and the hope (though you cannot presume)
    that something of all you come upon
    might find in you a local habitation.
I rounded a corner into the next room

and moved aside to let him pass,
    another coming toward me
    intent as I was, anxiety
and goodwill constant rivals in his face

through the long moment it took
　　to recognize him in the mirrored wall—
　　for there was no next room at all,
and I had met myself coming back.

from *Plume*

Aconite

◊   ◊   ◊

What's bane to wolves and whales
and poisons humans
nourishes the dot moth
and the yellow-tailed,

the wormwood pug, as dark
as a slug, the nervous
mouse moth, and the engrailed.
Distinguish milk-white

from ivory, learn to locate
sepals of aconite
from the trail: they resemble devils'
helmets one day

and, the next, the delicate cowls
Dominicans adjust
in prayer. No single apposition
fits, but, like a magnet,

pushes towards its opposite.
When the three-jawed dog
landed here, snarling at the sun
and pining for Hades,

his rabid sounds scattered
white foam,
drool which took root in Scythia
but flourished in areas

of higher rock, crag peaks
where nothing useful
bloomed, and no dust reached.
Now, down-creeping

into clearings, stalks wavering
along the tracks
that once linked factory towns,
the flower's grown

as inexorable as speech—
sustenance
or toxin, to anyone
who wanders close.

from *Raritan*

Using Black to Paint Light: Walking Through a Matisse Exhibit Thinking about the Arctic and Matthew Henson

◇   ◇   ◇

"The light range was so narrow if you exposed film for a white kid, the black kid sitting next to him would be rendered invisible except for the whites of his eyes and teeth. It was only when Kodak's two biggest clients—the confectionary and furniture industries—complained that dark chocolate and dark furniture were losing out that it came up with a solution."
—Broomberg and Chanarin

"When a contradiction is impossible to resolve except by a lie, then we know it is really a door."
—Simone Weil

I keep referring to the cold, as if that were the point.

Fact. Not point.

Forty-below was a good day. "In short, fine weather," you wrote once, before cutting out blocks of ice and fashioning another igloo for the whole crew each night.

But it isn't the point, that it was cold, is it?

How many days before arriving did you sit on the deck in that chair, staring out to sea, wearing a coarse blue shirt, the lost, well-mannered rhetoric of your day spiraling beneath a blue hat—concertina (at your ankle) outside the placid frame?

Thank you, whoever you are, for standing behind the camera and thinking "Matthew Henson" and "photograph" at the same time.

★

The unanticipated shock: so much believed to be white is actually—strikingly—blue. Endless blueness. White is blue. An ocean wave freezes in place. Blue. Whole glaciers, large as Ohio, floating masses of static water. All of them pale frosted azuls. It makes me wonder—yet again—was there ever such a thing as whiteness? I am beginning to grow suspicious. An open window.

I am blue.
I am a frozen blue ocean.
I am a wave struck cold in midair.
The wave is nude beneath her blue dress.
Her skin is blue.

★

To arrive in a place.

And this place in which you have arrived finally: a place you have always dreamt of arriving. Perhaps you have tried—for eighteen years—to get there, dreaming of landscapes, people, food. Always repulsed by your effort, unable to attain the trophy.

And then finally somehow you arrive one day and are immediately stunned because you realize more than anything, it isn't the landscape, food, the people. That thing which most astonishes you is the light, the way the air appears, how the sunlight hovers just before your eyes.

And you—then—wanting nothing more than to spend the day indoors watching the room. The vast ocean always nothing more than an open window. So you stay inside and choose to watch the same wall turn fifty reds, then later: slow, countless variations of blue. Blues you have never seen. There is a black beam overhead on the ceiling. Without it, the ability to see such light would disappear. The light is toying with you, and you like it. All of this because the darkness is now always overhead. That. That is what arriving means.

★

I want to say the same thing in a variety of different ways. Or I want to say many different things, but merely one way.

Perhaps there is only one word after all. Beneath all languages, beneath all other words: only one. Perhaps whenever we speak we are repeating it. All day long, the same single word over and over again.

★

Choose something dark. Choose a dark line to hang above you. If you want to see what light can do, always choose the dark.

★

Out on the ice, the light can blind you. The annals laced with men who set out without the protection of darkness. All finished blind.

Blackbirds, black bowhead whales, the raven, the night sky, the body inside, blue ink, pencil lead, chocolate, marzipan. Like us.

All water is a color. But what does that have to do with you and me, Matthew?

★

Maybe life is just this: walking with each other from one dark room to another. And looking.

Sometimes the paintings come to life. Sometimes you just love the word *pewter*. Sometimes the ocean waves at you. Sometimes there are goldfish in a jar. A bowl of oranges. Sometimes a woman steps down out of a frame and walks toward you. Sometimes she discards the white scarf, which covers her, and reveals her real body. Sometimes she leaves, moments later, covered in a striped jacket and leather hat.

Our lady of the dressing table.
Our lady of the rainy day.
Our lady of palm leaves, periwinkle, calla lilies.
Our lady of acanthus.
A garden redone three times.

★

Sometimes someone you love just falls through. Gone. The blue massive ridges of pressure shift, float away, move. Sometimes the ice breaks open. That's it. Sledge, dogs and all.

★

I fell through once. I'd grown cold, so I stood up and walked to get my coat. I was told it was hanging on the far wall of a very dark room. Because it was dark, I could see, really see—for the first time—how a particular gold thread sparkled on the collar. I reached out my hand. But before the wall, there was a large hole where stairs were being built, which I could not see. I walked into air and landed on my head. Underground.

Everything then turned a vivid black.

★

I wonder, Matthew, when you were out on the ice for years, trying very hard not to fall through, I wonder whether—like me—you ever thought of the same woman over and over again, whether you ever imagined her draped in a loose-fitting emerald robe, seated in a pink velvet chair, engulfed by a black so bright it was luminous?

I do.

Sometimes I lie here in bed before the fire, unable to move—this cane, this hideous cane, this glorious cane, cutting cane—and imagine that one particular curl falling forward toward her forehead. I imagine the same curl at this angle, then that. A recurring dream. When my bed becomes a vast field of frozen ice the color of indigo, and I cannot move, I begin to see her face. Each strand of her hair becomes a radiant small flame, twisting and burning so quietly. Then I look at your picture, you out on the ice, and I wonder if you ever feel like that, Matthew?

Like a woman, faceless and flung over
a desk, at rest or in tears, exquisite

quickly drawn ruffles about your shoulder,
halos of wide banana leaves

hovering just above your head?
Were there images you could not fling

from your mind? Events that clung
to you, coated you, repeating

themselves in a series: movements
or instruments in a symphony?

Objects that would not let you go:
an avocado tree; a certain street

at night where someone exceptionally kind
once took your arm as the two of you walked

along a wet sidewalk; trying
to remember the light on that certain gait:

your mother twirling a parasol, also walking
through a grove of olive trees?

Did you begin to find comfort
in the serial, the inexplicable and constant

reappearance of things, people, sensations,
every moment symphonically realized

and reentered. The way the days begin
to rhyme. Every moment

walking into the room again.
Sledge after sledge.

Matthew?

★

I fell through, into a hole in the floor. I landed far below, on my head. Sometimes I still forget my name. Sometimes I forget yours. Sometimes I forget how to spell *the*. Regularly I am unable to remember Adam Clayton Powell. Or how to conjugate *exist*. Sometimes I lie in bed and cannot feel my legs. It's like something quietly gnawed them off while I was in the kitchen making tea. From the knees down: this odd sensation, not nothing, but something, just not legs. If ice were not cold perhaps. Or the memory of a leg. I cannot feel my legs, but I can feel their memory.

In conversation, my face goes numb. It starts at my mouth and spreads out. When I am quiet it recedes. Why is numbness ascribed the color blue? It's not. It's red.

By the end of the day, my left hand has disappeared from the end of my arm. I ignore it. Hold my pen. Smile at you. What year is it, darling? I once lived where? With whom? Where is she now? What was her name?

★

I remember nurses. Their faces. Someone very, very kind—a woman—began to tape a pen inside my hand. I remember being suspended in a harness. Being lowered down into a warm blue pool. All the other patients there were very old. Here is how we all learned to walk properly again. Underwater. Blue.

Once I fell through—into the dark.

★

Braces and casts.

Being told not to write.

Being told not to read.

Forgetting someone I once promised I would never forget.

Remembering her finally, one year, then forgetting her again, the next day.

Remembering not remembering I'd forgotten.

Forgetting them completely.

★

When I look at photographs of Matisse, unable to walk, drawing on the wall from the bed, his charcoal tied to the end of a very long pole, I stop breathing.

Him, I think. Yes. I could marry him.

I could slip into his bed.

We could talk about real things.

I could be his dark line hovering above.

We could watch the light turning the room every color.

from *Gulf Coast*

First Christmas in the Village

◇   ◇   ◇

It was unanticipated, the birth,
and late at that, stormy and close,
as we were gathered in by the hearth.
Nothing about it called for words,
though the widow had no children
and taught a game with playing cards.

A fisherman brought an octopus
that sizzled on a metal grate
over the pulsing olive coals.
The widow's father leaned to the fire
and with a dark blade sawed off a leg
and laid it burning on my plate.

It tasted like a briny steak
with tentacles like tiny lips
oozing the savor of the sea,
my first octopus, its brain afire.
And the illicit cards—*Don't tell the priest*—
a wink at caution in the game of living.

That night all human struggle ended,
or recollection wants it so.
That night all murders were forgotten
in the salt abundance and the storm
and the warm fire in the widow's house
when the vast peace was said to be born.

That night I carried a bucket of coals
back to my rented dwelling, wind
trailing the fading sparks behind—
a small fire, for the warmth it made
as the stars held steady in the dome,
and sleep became an open grave.

from *The New Criterion*

ROBERT MORGAN

Window

◊   ◊   ◊

There is a kind of oak, a black
or maybe Spanish oak, whose leaves
turn only after a hard freeze
to reddish orange with just a hint
of silver in the sheen, so subtle,
unique, you have to stop and drink
it in among the now bare woods.
The color might be something in
a chapel tower, above an altar,
a place to pause and to attend,
beyond the cattails in the ditch,
the dying weeds, the rotting mulch.

from *Southern Poetry Review*

Invitation

◊   ◊   ◊

Come in, come in—the water's fine! You can't get lost here—even
if you wanted to hide behind a clutch of spiny oysters. I'll find you.
     If you ever leave me at night, by boat—you'll see
          the arrangement of golden sun stars in a sea of milk

and though it's tempting to visit them—stay. I've been trained
to look up and up all my life, no matter the rumble on earth
     but I've learned it's okay to glance down once in a while
          into the sea. So many lessons bubble up if you just know

where to look. Clouds of plankton hurricaning in open
whale mouths will send you east and chewy urchins will slide
     you west. Squid know how to be rich with ten
          empty arms. There are humans who don't know the feel

of a good bite and embrace at least once a day. Underneath
you, narwhals spin upside down while their singular tooth needles
     you like a compass pointed toward home. Deep where
          imperial volutes and hatchetfish live, colors humans have

not yet named glow in caves made from black coral and clamshell.
A giant squid finally let itself be captured in a photograph
     and the paper nautilus ripple-flashes scarlet and two kinds
          of violet when it silvers you near. Who knows what

will happen next? If you still want to look up, I hope you see
the dark sky as oceanic, boundless, limitless—like all
the shades of blue revealed in a glacier. Let's listen
how this planet hums with so much wing, fur, and fin.

from *Poetry*

B.F.F.

◇ ◇ ◇

I lie in the dark & stretch the portrait
of a white woman across my face
until it splits. Beneath my bed, a catalogue
of half-faced women sing me to sleep.
I'll start with Amanda Elias
& how I thought, in order to be worthy
of desire, I had to wear her skin.
For four years I sat across from her
in the lunchroom, mimicked her posture
blinked when she did, became the mirror
so concerned with the rise & fall
of each one of her blemishes
I even took her to the winter formal
watched, in the green glow of the gymnasium
at how I—she danced, chiffon willow
silk mystic. I watched how the boys held her
whispered a joke in her ear that made me laugh.
Stupid boys. Stupidstupid boys.
I tell the man in the chatroom
I am a platter of soft curls. Send him her photo.
Crack an egg & remove the yolk.
He could marry me, you know? You don't.
She would never. Once, after another heartbreak
she came to school with cuts on her wrist
& maybe my rage was out of concern—I was
after all, a great friend, unflinching in my kindness
or maybe I hated how ungrateful she was
or maybe I thought her technique was pathetic
horizontal, barely breaking the first layer

or maybe I wanted a bigger opening
to attach a zipper, slip on her hand-me-downs
& somehow she must've known all along
her body was a dress I hung for motivation
the way she cried while I held her wrist
dabbing it with cold water, inspecting the damage
how she kept on saying, *Sorry. Sorry.*

from *BuzzFeed*

ALFRED NICOL

Addendum

◇　◇　◇

Give to Caesar what is his,
namely, everything there is.
I see a lot of eyebrows raised.
Let's check the books. You'll be amazed.

An x. An o. A hug and kiss.
Render unto Caesar this.

Render unto Caesar that.
His the dog, his the cat.

Render up your reading time.
Render, too, your reverie.

Render up the uphill climb,
render what you hope to be.

If God is dead, does Caesar get
the flip side of the coin? You bet!

Render up. You'll never win.
The croupier will rake it in.

Caesar's arms are open wide;
your whole estate will fit inside.

from *First Things*

Skin Deep

◇   ◇   ◇

Pardon the black water
in the sink, restless &
tyrannical in its wading.
The plate's shellacked
face folds into my own,
reflects another face I
have inherited these past
few years. The faucet
runs endlessly, so fluid
with brisk pace, it seems
to almost be entering the
mouth of which it exits.
I look into the water, now
blackened from a series
of elements like foam &
foreign liquid making its
home in this metal bowl,
factory of carved ceramics
& glass forms. I heard the
spoon bends when we can
deny its existence but of
course you can't deny this:
Race, so permanent upon
ourselves, it becomes our
own tombstone with names.
I once tried to drown my
skin & be human without it.
Jump in, said the knife &
I did, through the soap, slick

debris of white foam, glazing
this fine black creek. I dived
skin first, then the body,
wading, wading, waiting
for something to clean me.

from *The Adroit Journal*

S H E A N A   O C H O A

Hands

◊   ◊   ◊

I see them daily managing their way
around my body, my house, the pages
I turn. Hands of my father, sinewy
and scarred, they splinter the cold.
Hands of my mother, feline
and fearless, they wade the moon's
pools. With age I have noticed cracks
overcrowding the skin. Perhaps
there was a time when my fingers
awoke spring petals from hibernation,
crafted Nahuatlan sundials, slayed
minotaur charging by the sea.
There is a map in the seat of my palm
—a plan of a city I've never been,
instructions to the lost poetry
of Sappho, or a codified explanation
for the Milky Way—but a wheat
brown mole covers the key.

from *Catamaran*

Silver Spoon Ode

◇   ◇   ◇

I was born with a silver spoon in my mouth
and a silver knife, and a silver fork.
I would complain about it—the spoon was not greasy,
it tasted like braces, my shining access
to cosmetic enhancement. And I complained about
the taste of my fillings in my very expensive
mouth, as if only my family was paying—
where did I think the rich got
their money but from everyone else?
My mother beat me in 4/4 time,
and I often, now, rant to her beat—I wear
her rings as if I killed her for them, as my
people killed, and climbed up over
the dead. And I sound as if I am bragging
about it. I was born with a spoon instead of a
tongue in my mouth—dung spoon,
diamond spoon. And who would I be
to ask for forgiveness? I would be a white girl.
And I hear Miss Lucille, as if on the mountain
where I'd stand beside her, and brush away the insects,
and sometimes pick one off her, sometimes
by the wings, and toss it away. And Lucille
is saying, to me, You have asked for enough,
and been given in excess. And that thing in your mouth,
open your mouth and let that thing go,
let it fly back into the mine where it was brought
up from the underworld at the price of

lives, beloved lives. And now,
enough, Shar, now a little decent silence.

from *The Nation*

Tilia cordata

◇   ◇   ◇

Here, near the desert, the air's so dry
even the scent of lilac and peony

won't carry very far. And they've been gone
for a good few weeks now. It's the end of June,

the foothills' transitory emerald
now scorched to a stubborn, bleached-out gold,

the mountains incoherent without snow.
The breeze, sporadic at best, unloading cargo

just to stay afloat, quickly abandons
any pretense of carrying a scent. Only the lindens

(a whim of early dreamers on my street)
from some inner surge of altruism, conceit

or pure naiveté, choose just this instant
to loose, en masse, their all-consuming scent.

I could spend its all too brief duration
just sitting on my porch, breathing it in.

My neighbor hates it—says it's too much—
but my Russian house cleaners used to harvest a batch

of the tiny flowers every summer for tea
prized all over Europe as a delicacy:

in French, it's *tilleul*, the very tisane
that, moistening a random madeleine,

inspired Proust's obsession with *Lost Time*.
It's a main ingredient in Sleepytime

and the *tè per i nervi e per insonnia*
I used to drink in Italy. *Tilia cordata*

is the Latin name, both for tree and flower.
In England it's *lime* (Coleridge's *bower*

hardly a *prison*), its unparalleled
heart-shaped leaves the first green to unfold

in spring, in autumn, the last to fall.
But its best feature, of course, is the spell

cast by its fragrance every June.
A pity this often happens when I'm gone

doing the "research" my daughters call a scam
since it usually involves extracting a poem

from some longed-for place, or, sometimes, two.
Three years ago, in search of art nouveau,

I scoured Barcelona, Nancy, Glasgow,
and a section of Darmstadt called Mathildenhöe,

once a *Jugendstil* (art nouveau in German) colony.
I'd never before traveled to Germany

and though I loved each *Jugendstil* detail,
was perpetually uneasy, every guttural

a broken razor blade inside my mouth.
I suppose it was inevitable: the birth-

right of a Jew born in 1956
to parents still reeling from the war's aftershocks.

I have no memory
of a time before I'd heard the word *Nazi*—

always sotto voce, in that nervous hiss
my mother reserved for fatal illness

or—on rare occasions—the obscene.
My earliest recollections from a screen:

Old Yeller, Walter Cronkite, *Pinocchio*
and piles of gaunt bodies in a backhoe,

being shoveled—human bodies—into ditches.
I badgered my mother after hearing snatches

of unassimilable whispered conversation
and wouldn't take a shower until I was seven,

worried gas might come out. That's what my mother
had told me: *gas came out instead of water*

when pressed for what those whispers meant.
Needless to say, I thought it was an accident,

that a malfunctioning shower might cause my death.
Even now, I still prefer a bath

though I know the showers themselves were not at fault.
just as—circumambulating Darmstadt,

in search of still more feats of art nouveau—
it's not as if I didn't know

that the people I saw around me were far too young
for incrimination, their German tongue

a way of putting things like any other.
But though I learn quickly, my entire repertoire

was *ein cappuccino bitte* and *danke schön*
and even uttering those sounds felt like treason.

I decided to go Worms—where the great Rashi
—a Rabbinic wonder—had gone to study

in the eleventh century—
a forty-minute train ride away

but, en route to the station, as I imagined
asking for the *Jüdisches Museum*, I turned around.

In that setting, the two-word phrase
seemed to sum up the whole dread enterprise:

reducing *Jüdisches* to a *Museum*.
I couldn't bear to utter its name,

much less actually to go there
though I owe to Rashi my first glimmer

of the endless acrobatic feats of words,
their mutability, the daredevil speeds

with which they abolish time and distance.
He could find, behind the most straightforward utterance,

an implicit labyrinthine universe
and another behind that. (At issue was Genesis

chapter 27, verse 19:
fourth-grade Hebrew School with Mrs. Gelman.)

I didn't need a Rashi Museum; I had his commentary.
What I needed was another history

or at least a place where mine was less conspicuous;
but my train was a day away. I wandered, aimless

till I remembered reading about a *Jugendstil* gate
to the park at the end of town and then forgot

architecture in a stunning crush of green
expansive trees extending on and on,

so thrilling, after years in an arid climate,
like Philly's Fairmount Park—my father's favorite—

where the surrounding city seemed a shrill mistake
at least to a little girl riding piggyback

through the park her father had wandered as a boy.
In Darmstadt, of all places, his fifty-year-old joy

was newly palpable, though I now wondered
if he hadn't in fact felt a bit bewildered

at being in that spot and fully grown,
as I've always felt when I've brought my children

to my old beloved childhood haunts.
Maybe you're more susceptible in strange environments?

How could a German park bring me my father?
But sometimes what's familiar is so familiar

ubiquity becomes its camouflage;
you don't distinguish it, don't acknowledge

its presence where it doesn't quite belong;
I'm not sure when I realized that all along

I'd been breathing in the smell of linden,
more intense than on my street, the very linden

that kept me on my porch for hours dreaming.
And while it's not really that surprising—

isn't *Unter den Linden*
the most famous thoroughfare in Berlin?—

that a huge German park would smell like linden
on the final afternoon of June,

I—unhinged already—was undone,
as if the trees themselves were in collusion

to throw me off completely. How could this
thoroughly alien, unnerving place

have anything in common with my home?
Was it a sign? If so, from whom?

And what, exactly, was it saying?
Not that it mattered. I wasn't listening.

It was hard enough dealing with the fragrance,
much less good and evil, guilt and innocence,

which I knew—in any case—are not confined
to a single unlucky piece of land.

But the obvious wasn't obvious in that place;
my principles—such as they were—were powerless

in the face of the matter-of-fact harmony
in evidence around me. Shouldn't Germany

be paralyzed by its hideous statistics?
How could any person reconcile such facts

a mere sixty-eight years further on?
Still, it's a lifetime. And we just have one.

That is, if it isn't ripped away from us.
But mine—by the narrow grace

of eleven years and (some time before that)
a shtetl subsistence so inadequate

it sent my four grandparents across an ocean—
is still intact. Surely, its duration

ought to be directed toward what's beautiful,
my linden this very instant casting its spell,

its outspread branches almost at my porch.
And I'm here for once, within the reach

of its thick, evocative perfume,
an all-encompassing amalgam

of itself and every time I've breathed it in:
my daughters babies, or little children

pointing their fingers and exulting *tree*
then *bird*, then *linden*, then *black-capped chickadee*,

my ex-husband my husband and still alive
or me: disoriented, restive

bolstered by a welcome shock of green
until I realize something like this very linden

must have been attendant on atrocity.
Surely, if not in Darmstadt, then in another city

(Warsaw? Paris? Amsterdam? Berlin?)
some of those millions were smelling linden—

given the tree's prevalence, its heavy fragrance—
as they were being herded onto trains?

My daughters have been known to make bets
before dinner parties about how many minutes

will pass before I bring up the Holocaust.
(You're an easy target when you're obsessed;

usually, the winning number's about twenty.)
They're merciless, my girls, if extremely funny

and hardly oblivious of horror.
But they really do think I'm in error;

my narrowness and bias inexcusable.
And I'm weirdly proud of their disapproval.

Let's hope their view won't require accommodation;
but if, in time, it does, no doubt, *their* children

will call them on it, as well they should.
Surely it can't be good

to infuse one of Earth's loveliest offerings—
a linden tree in June—with human beings

at their very basest. Something's wrong with me.
Not to mention that my reasoning is faulty.

No one in that appalling circumstance
could pay any attention to a fragrance

and even if they did, who's to say
whether it caused—by brutal contrast—agony

or offered, one last time, a tiny balm?
It's so far beyond me. I'm safe at home

breathing in the fragrance from my tree,
an exquisite, if no longer entirely

untroubled or uncomplicated pleasure.
But doesn't every good thing have its measure

of imperfection lurking in the wings?
The glass we're obliged to break at weddings

to acknowledge the Holy Temple's destruction?
In a world this damaged, this out of proportion,

what remains untouched? Nothing at all.
Still, who can blame me if I stay awhile?

It can't last too much longer, this perfume,
but here, just now, my linden tree's in bloom.

from *The Antioch Review*

Sad Math

◊   ◊   ◊

My last cellmate had only a fifth-grade education.
His name was Larry
and he had undiagnosed dyslexia and developmental delays.

He reminded me of my big sister DeeDee, who died
long before I understood the futility
of blaming the sick for being ill.

Larry liked to play a game I couldn't stand,
but I felt sorry for him, so I would play along.

"Celly," he'd call, "they take 55% for restitution, right?"
"Yeah," I'd reply.
"And my papers say I owe $9,000 right?"
"Yeah."
"So if my family sends me $1,500, how much that leaves me?"
Closing my eyes, I do the math.
"$675"
"That should take care of me for awhile, right Celly?"
"Yeah, Larry, that will last you awhile."

After that, Larry would get quiet, settle back on his bunk
and stare at our empty lockers with a simple little smile.
I knew he was imagining what they would look like full.

Sometimes he'd fill out commissary lists for the prison store,
the care package ordering forms,
revising them daily, weighing his choices at just below a whisper.

The amounts Larry wanted and calculated varied a lot
but were always outrageous: two, six, ten thousand dollars.

I pretended I didn't notice that his family never wrote,
and that he never received any packages or money.

from *The Way Back*

The Week Before She Died

◇   ◇   ◇

I dream us young, again,
mother and daughter back
on 69th Street inside
our old brownstone—across
from the church, patch of lawn—

a house neglected, wrecked,
as if the family
had been forced at gunpoint
to move away. In corners
dirt stacked like minuscule

anthills; along the edges
of room—crumpled clothes, bodiless;
littered across the floor
dry-cleaning bags, vestiges
of what they once protected.

A Turkish scarf, embroidered
with sequins, glitter, beads,
tantalizes. My mother
holds it close, says, "You should
wear it." The doorbell rings.

At the top of the stairs
he waits for us to answer.
My mother's ballet partner,
Russian, stows something covert
behind his almond eyes. With three

regal strides he commands
our gaze, pronounces the red
brocade robe his, lofts high
the scarf, the sash he flung
in *Giselle*, circling the empty

living room. With mischief he bows
low before my mother. Her love
for him, a mountain. The doorbell
chimes. A blond, blue-eyed dancer,
in epaulets, arrives.

She straightens shoulders, turns,
walks away. Rudy asks
Erik, "Did you ever tell her
about us?" No response. The secrets
men keep, my mother knows.

from *Virginia Quarterly Review*

Bells' Knells

◇   ◇   ◇

My hands fold again and again into prayer shapes:
a steeple, an angel, your face's sharp angles. You strung

all our hopes from the rafters of structures: this gothic,
that Catholic, this cracked brick, that basement.

Your promise: a ticking, a lingering wish
that persists on each altar, each future that falters.

You did the exalting. God did the exacting. Redacting
your afternoons, vestments and basements; your words

cold and keyhole, steel and exact. A harp's not real singing,
this dirge never could hold you back, and the church just

a beautiful stack of shellacked, painted marble
and wood. What good that we're here, singing hymns,

when in weeks or in months you'll recall that ripe
fruit in the mouth is worth salt in the wound.

We both knelt at the pew.
We both knew we were doomed.

from *Smartish Pace*

Happy Birthday, Herod

◇   ◇   ◇

Like always, Herod's birthday is today,
and I can hear the tambourine
brioso. I can hear the oboe skirl.
Like always, Salome
is getting down to business, veil by veil.
Her eyes are green;
all other eyes, obscene
ravishers of a writhing girl,
are piercing what is see-through anyway.

Like always, without fail,
something repulsive has been done:
under the Dead Sea sun
another sort of flesh
(that corpse I mean, the headless one)
is summoning the blowflies—fresh
gratification for a mother's grudge.

Like always, who am I to judge?
Indifferent to whatever moral thing
a servant might be carrying
around the party on a tray,
I stand with stiff voyeurs
devouring those curves of hers,
worshipping the elastic,
the orgastic,
Salome.

Forgive me: Herod's birthday is today.

from *The New Criterion*

RUBEN QUESADA

Angels in the Sun

◊   ◊   ◊

after Turner

I would have waited alone a thousand
years for the coming of angels,
blinding bright as the spring sun to arrive,

to abandon this world for another.
Stunned by their flashing lights aflame

across the bow of their space craft—landing

lights for that world. Herds of animals:
horses, humans, and fish fixed.
The angels approached.

Come angels! Come beasts!
Men and women cried out
to each other; the angels cried;

some were lost between their earthly life

and paradise and what is paradise, anyway?
Few imagined being bound to this world;

blue halo of emerald mountains;
extraordinary, ordinary—they rose,

a crucifixion yardarm flying away.

from *The American Poetry Review*

La Mano

◇   ◇   ◇

For the more than 60,000 children from Central America who cross the border unaccompanied.

With lines from Maya Angelou and Richard Wilbur.

Arcing above our apartment building,
     above the rousing city and green skirts
of the San Salvador volcano, a flock
     of wild parakeets comes to roost
outside our window; my nine-month son
     rests his head on my chest and all I want
is to draw the curtains, but he's coughed
     all night and now his breathing
is slow, near sleep, though his eyes snap open
     with each squawk. I imagine the parakeets
preening their emerald feathers, joyful in their ceremony
     of clacks and trills. They are not musing
the capriciousness of nature as I am; they don't know
     five-thirty a.m., only that the sun has tinged
the mountainsides gold and that this alcove echoes
     their welcome beautifully. The wild parakeets tap
at the windowpane and my son stirs,
     raises his sleep-etched face to mine.
Together we slip past the curtain and discover
     seven green parakeets, perhaps a little smaller,
their feathers scruffier than I had envisioned.
     Two squabble over a prime niche and the stronger
one comes towards the glass, wings unfurled,
     fat tongue thrusting from his open beak. I want

to unlatch the window and sprinkle seed, lure them
        to perch on our shoulders and arms, anything
to make them stay longer. Instead, my son, rooted in
        the things unknown but longed for still—
greets them with the slap of an open palm to the windowpane,
        and in a clapping of wings
they leap from the narrow corridor at once, a raucous fleeing,
        with headlong and unanimous consent,
a disappearing stain, a distant murmuration
        swallowed from sight.

from *Green Mountains Review*

PAISLEY REKDAL

Philomela

◇   ◇   ◇

Because her grandmother loved
the arts, her father said, she'd willed
the money to a distant cousin
working as a sculptor. A decision
made the month before she'd died
from cancer, which the young woman
cannot now believe was due
only to a brain tumor, having endured
the last, deliberate ways her grandmother asked
why she'd never married.
The cousin, who inherited the money,
showed her sculptures in a converted barn:
the only space large enough to contain
the seething shapes that seemed to flame
up from their pedestals
in precarious arcs. An audacity
of engineering the young woman
tried not to see as a reproach
when, curious, she visited:
how the sculptures made her feel
too earth-bound, solid. At the gallery,
she stared a long while at what she thought
was a tree blasted by lightning,
but the more she looked, the more clearly
shapes emerged. There
were a man's hands gripping a slender figure
by the waist, the thin body writhing,
frozen in his arms. It was
a girl, she saw, with shredded

bark for breasts and dark charred wood
for legs, as if the limbs had been snatched
from a fire while burning.
Her twig hands raked
her captor's face. The young woman
could read no emotion on it,
however: the plank face
had been scraped clean; all the fear
and anger burned instead inside
their twisting bodies: she could see
the two there stuck at a point
of perfect hatred for each other: she
for his attack, he for her resistance,
perhaps the beauty he could not
stand in her, as her last date in college
had hissed, "You think
you're so fucking pretty," spitting it
into her face so that she'd had to turn
her cheek to wipe it, which was when
he'd grabbed her arm then, pinning her—

Was this why her cousin had been chosen, to make
what she'd had no words for?
Persephone, the piece she stood
amazed before had been titled: the last,
unconscious gift of her grandmother.
"For your wedding," she'd said
her last week, pointing
to her own open palm in which
nothing rested. Perhaps
her grandmother had imagined
a gold ring there. Perhaps a string
of thick pink pearls. The young woman
drove home from the gallery, took a shower,
and did not tell anyone that day
what it was she'd seen. A month later,
in the mail, a package came
from her father: her grandmother's Singer
sewing machine, its antique brass wheel
scrubbed of gold, the wooden handle

glossy with vines of mother-of-pearl.
It was lovely, and for a moment
she considered sewing a quilt with it,
onto which she might embroider
shooting stars in reds and saffron, the figure
of a child, perhaps, or of a man
by a house's courtyard, his hat
in his hands, his broad body
naked, harmless.

How much thread would that take
to make? she wondered. And considered it
a long while before packing up
the machine again, sliding it back
into its wood crate and high up onto a shelf
of her basement closet. The place
she kept her college books and papers,
where she told herself it could wait.

from *Narrative*

Walkman

◇   ◇   ◇

I didn't mean to quit drinking,
it just sort of happened.
I'd always assumed
it'd be difficult, or not
difficult, exactly,
but impossible.
Then one New Year's Eve
twenty years ago
at the VFW, Craig and I
were drinking beer
from brown bottles,
peeling the labels off
into little confetti nests.
In Mexico
the previous New Year's Eve,
I'd started drinking
again after a year sober.
I traveled by myself
in Oaxaca for a month
and had at least two
beautiful experiences.
The bus I was on broke
down in the mountains
and I watched the stars blink
on with a Mexican girl
who later sent me a letter
I never answered. That's one
of the experiences. The others
are secrets. We left the VFW

at a reasonable hour for once.
I never took another drink.
I'm not sure why not.
I don't think it had anything
to do with me. I think
it was a miracle. Like when
the hero at the last
second pulls the lever to switch
the train to the track the heroine's
not tied to. I was always broke
in those days, whereas now I'm just
poor. I brought a Walkman
and a backpack stuffed with
cassettes to Oaxaca. I was sick
of them all within a week
and longed to buy a new tape
but couldn't spare the pesos.
I listened to *Live Through This*
at the Zapotec ruins
of Monte Albán,
Rumours on the bus to DF.
At Puerto Ángel,
my headphones leaking
tinny discord
across a rooftop bar,
I sat watching the ocean.
An American man about the age
I am now
asked me what I was listening to.
I said Sonic Youth. He asked
which album, I said *Sister*.
He chuckled and said
"I'm Johnny Strike."
It probably wasn't a miracle,
but I couldn't believe it.
Here was the guy who wrote
Crime's 1976 classic
"Hot Wire My Heart,"
which Sonic Youth covered
on their 1987 classic, *Sister*,

which I was listening to
on my Walkman
at the end of Mexico in the sun.
Except actually I was
listening to *Daydream Nation*,
I change it to *Sister*
when I tell that story.
But it's a beautiful story
even without embellishment.
That's another of the Oaxacan
experiences I mentioned,
but the rest are secrets.
Oh Mexico, as James Schuyler
wrote to Frank O'Hara,
are you just another
dissembling dream?
Schuyler was too tender
for me then, but now
he is just tender enough.
I love his wishes.
That "the beautiful humorous
white whippet" could
be immortal, for instance.
But I can't always forgive
his Central Park West tone,
his Austrian operettas
and long long lawns,
though he wasn't rich
and was tormented
enough, God knows.
In the summer of 1984
in Salida, Colorado,
I had Slade and Steve Perry
on my Walkman.
I drank milk from jumbo
Burger King glasses
emblazoned with scenes
from *Return of the Jedi*.
You can't buy tampons
with food stamps

even if your mother
insists that you try.
Salida sits along
the Arkansas River,
whose current
one hot afternoon
swept me away
and deposited me
in a shallow far downstream.
It was the first time
I thought I was going
to die and didn't. The Arkansas
and everything else are mortal.
My mom had been born again,
to my chagrin. But lately I find
I do believe in God
the Father Almighty, Maker
of heaven and earth:
and in Jesus Christ,
his Son our Lord,
who was conceived by
the Holy Ghost. How
the hell did I become
a Christian? Grace,
I guess. It just sort of
happened. I admit I find
the resurrection of the body
and life everlasting
difficult, or not difficult,
exactly, but impossible.
There is no crazier belief
than that we won't be
covered by leaves, leaves,
leaves, as Schuyler has it,
which is to say, really gone,
as O'Hara put it in his lovely
sad poem to John Ashbery.
But hope is a different animal
from belief. "The crazy hope
that Paul proclaims in 2

Corinthians," my friend John
wrote to me when his mother
died. The Christian religion
is very beautiful sometimes
and very true at other times,
though sophisticated persons
are still expected to be above
all that sort of thing. Well,
I'm a Marxist
too. Go and sell that thou
hast, and give to the poor.
On his new album Dr. Dre
says "Anybody complaining
about their circumstances
lost me." At the risk of losing
more billionaires, complain
about your circumstances,
I say. I listened to *The Chronic*
on my Walkman the summer
I worked the night shift
at Kinko's. I was dating Deirdre,
who when I placed my headphones
on her ears and pushed play
said "Why is this man cursing
at me?" Said it more loudly
than was strictly necessary.
A crazy man
would come into Kinko's
around two A.M. and ask me
to fax dire, scribbled warnings
to every news outlet in Denver.
He wanted to let people know
that God would punish the area
with natural disasters
if the county succeeded
in evicting him from the land
he was squatting on. He'd ask me
to help him think of various
extreme weather events
that God might unleash.

I'd say "Typhoons?"
though we were in Colorado.
He'd scribble typhoons.
Scraps of dirty paper absolutely
covered front and back with ominous,
angrily scrawled black characters:
ATTN. NBC NIGHTLY NEWS THERE WILL
BE FIRES TORNADOES TYPHOONS.
I would help him compose his screeds
then fax each one to Denver's
major TV and radio stations, *The Denver Post*,
and the *Rocky Mountain News*,
which has since stopped its presses
for good. Except in fact I would
only pretend to fax them
and then refuse his money,
saying I was glad to help the cause.
What if he wasn't batshit but a true
prophet? The Denver metropolitan area
was not visited by disaster
at that time, but this proves
nothing. Look at Jonah and
Nineveh, that great city.
I don't believe he was a prophet,
but Kinko's is beautiful
at two A.M. even if I hated
working there. The rows
of silent copiers
like retired dreadnoughts
in a back bay, the fluorescent
pallor, the classic-rock station
I would turn back up after
my coworker turned it down.
Did the guy sketch amateurish
floods, tornadoes, etc.,
on his jeremiads or did I
imagine that? I wish
I'd thought to make copies
for myself. I wish I'd kept
the Mexican girl's letter.

I wish I'd kept the copiers
with their slow arms
of light, the lights of DF
filling the Valley of Mexico
as the bus makes its slow way
down and Stevie sings what you
had, oh, what you lost. Schuyler
and his wishes! "I wish it was
1938 or '39 again." "I wish
I could take an engine apart
and reassemble it." "I wish I'd
brought my book of enlightening
literary essays." "I wish I could press
snowflakes in a book like flowers."
That last one's my favorite. I wish
I'd written it. I would often kick
for months until driven back to a bar
by fear or boredom or both. I saw
Tomorrow Never Dies—starring
Pierce Brosnan, the second-worst
James Bond—in Oaxaca and
came out wishing my life were
romantic and exciting and charmed
or at least that I had someone
to talk to. So I stopped at the first
bar I saw, and someone
talked to me. It's so sad and
perfect to be young and alone
in the Zócalo when the little lights
come up like fish surfacing
beneath the moon and you want
to grab the people walking by
and say who are you, are you
as afraid as I am. And you don't
know that twenty years later
you'll be writing this poem.
Well, now I'm being sentimental
and forgetting that in those days
I wrote the worst poems ever.
"I held a guitar and trembled

and would not sing" is an actual
line I wrote! The typhoon guy
could have written better poetry.
Today I want to write about
how it's been almost twenty years
since I owned a Walkman.
Just think: there was a song
that I didn't know
would be the last song
I would ever play on a Walkman.
I listened to it like it was just
any old song,
because it was.

from *The Paris Review*

Personae Who Got Loose

◇   ◇   ◇

Aloof, wary, notwithstanding her giddy enthusiasm for handsome misogynists and fine crystal.

So cavalier and mischievous, no one noticed that he never drank more than one glass of anything.

Anxious, extremely frugal man who lavishes every third paycheck on a charity for children in Nicaragua.

At four years she could not enjoy the ride on her carousel pony, angrily rocking and urging it forward against the pole to go faster.

He was a veteran zen buddhist with a hankering for Mounds Bars and women with multiple tattoos.

She drove a pickup and walked a muzzled Doberman, and any day of the week could fall apart completely over Greta Garbo love scenes.

Nonchalance was his middle name, in spite of his serially intense devotion to his mother's boyfriends.

The stage was full of splinters and dog hair, but people liked to lie down naked on it anyway.

from *Copper Nickel*

Genesis

◊   ◊   ◊

Oh, I said, this is going to be.
And it was.
Oh, I said, this will never happen.
But it did.
And a purple fog descended upon the land.
The roots of trees curled up.
The world was divided into two countries.
Every photograph taken in the first was of people.
Every photograph taken in the second showed none.
All of the girl children were named And.
All of the boy children named Then.

from *Poetry*

KAY RYAN

Some Transcendent Addiction
to the Useless

◇ ◇ ◇

—George Steiner, *The Poetry of Thought*

Unlike the
work of
most people
you're supposed
to unthread
the needle.
It will be
a lifetime
task, far
from simple:
the empty eye
achievable—
possibly—but
it's going
to take
fake sewing
worthy of
Penelope.

from *Parnassus: Poetry in Review*

We'll Always Have Parents

◊   ◊   ◊

It isn't what he said in *Casablanca*
and it isn't strictly true. Nonetheless
we'll always have them, much as we have Paris.
They're in our baggage, or perhaps *are* baggage
of the old-fashioned type, before the wheels,
which we remember when we pack for Paris.
Or don't remember. Paris doesn't know
if you're thinking of it. Neither do your parents,
although they'll say you ought to visit more,
as if they were as interesting as Paris.
Both Paris and your parents are as dead
and as alive as what's inside your head.
Meanwhile, those lovers, younger every year
(because with every rerun we get older),
persuade us less, for all their cigarettes
and shining unshed tears about the joy
of Paris blurring in their rearview mirror,
that they've surpassed us in sophistication.
Granted, they were born before our parents
but don't they seem by now, Bogart and Bergman,
like our own children? Think how we could help!
We could ban their late nights, keep them home
the whole time, and prevent their ill-starred romance!
Here's looking at us, Kid. You'll thank your parents.

from *The Common*

Voxel

◇ ◇ ◇

O newest of new words,
welcome to my mouth!

Though you are still not
in the dictionary (yet),

you are transparent in meaning:
a pixel with volume,

the basic unit of 3-D
printing, and now that we have

you, voxel, Plato will have
to let us back in his Republic

because we can print beds
and guns and pots and pans

and for so long, we thought
that nothing could be imagined

until it was imagined by us;
and if now, like those monks

in that story, where they
end the world by finding

every possible arrangement
for the letters in the name

of God, we too can see
everything that can ever

be photographed
or represented visually,

at least to the sighted,
then pixels mean

that we can predict
every thing that might

ever be seen by creating
an algorithm to generate

every permutation of every
image that could ever

be arranged out of pixels
and yes, the permutations

are so many as to be infinite
for all practical purposes

because we die, because
we can more easily calculate

the number of possibilities
than actually look at them,

and yes, this was always
in our eyes, because pixels

are merely externalized
rods and cones

but still, every single one
of those possibilities is there

in that algorithm, or in the
idea of that algorithm,

and you, little voxel,
are still a primitive thing,

a gradation so coarse as to
evoke *Donkey Kong* in

its earliest days
of blocky charm,

but refinement
is our human skill,

so much more so
than love or penmanship

or peacemaking, at which
we have learned little, but now,

voxel, everything is contained
inside you—not fire

perhaps—but our model
of fire—not affection,

perhaps—but our model
of affection, and dear voxel,

the smaller your become,
the more powerful you will be.

Dear voxel, already
I am beginning to think

of myself in terms of you,
and sweet voxel, the day

is coming when I will print
my selfies as tiny dioramas

made of you, and you will know
that you contain all

that is human
in the universe,

that you hold everything
in versatile potential,

my neurons, my face,
my planet, my stem cells,

my lover, my spaceship,
my coffin, my poems,

my eyesight, my corpse.

from *The Literary Review*

NICOLE SEALEY

A Violence

◊ ◊ ◊

You hear the high-pitched yowls of strays
fighting for scraps tossed from a kitchen window.
They sound like children you might have had.
Had you wanted children. Had you a maternal bone,
you would wrench it from your belly and fling it
from your fire escape. As if it were the stubborn
shard now lodged in your wrist. No, you would hide it.
Yes, you would hide it inside a barren nesting doll
you've had since you were a child. Its smile
reminds you of your father, who does not smile.
Nor does he believe you are his. "You look just like
your mother," he says, "who looks just like a fire
of suspicious origin." A body, I've read, can sustain
its own sick burning, its own hell, for hours.
It's the mind. It's the mind that cannot.

from *The New Yorker*

Advent

◊　◊　◊

His mother must have looked away,
the reckless boy who teeters on
the railing of the balcony.

Beneath him, the congregation sings
a final hymn in a minor key.

Above, the oculus, gold leaf,
the folded wings of Gabriel.

Impossible to say what lured
him from his seat—the choir's appeal
or the angel's feet?
                    What is his name
so we might call him, safely, down—
this child who balances between

what cannot and what can be seen,
the martyrs and the marbled ground?

from *The Sewanee Review*

Dispatch from Midlife

◊   ◊   ◊

Gender is the civic center
of my adrenal gland.
I am bound by certainty
to keep it in a shell.
Past fertility, insomnia
is the new membrane
around my nights. My
mortal terror is the now
with what's left of me.
What are you, demand
the witches from the throne
of their own infallible
femininity. I'm a monster
of my own making who quit
one guile for this new one,
wanton with indifference.

from *Colorado Review*

TRACY K. SMITH

An Old Story

◇　◇　◇

We were made to understand it would be
Terrible. Every small want, every niggling urge,
Every hate swollen to a kind of epic wind.

Livid, the land, and ravaged, like a rageful
Dream. The worst in us having taken over
And broken the rest utterly down.

                              A long age
Passed. When at last we knew how little
Would survive us—how little we had mended

Or built that was not now lost—something
Large and old awoke. And then our singing
Brought on a different manner of weather.

Then animals long believed gone crept down
From trees. We took new stock of one another.
We wept to be reminded of such color.

from *The Nation*

Why California Will Never Be Like Tuscany

◇   ◇   ◇

There must have been huge oaks and pines, cedars,
              maybe madrone,
in Tuscany and Umbria long ago.
A few centuries after wood was gone, they began to build with brick and stone.

Brick and stone farm houses, solid, fireproof,
steel shutters and doors.

But farming changed.
Sixty thousand vacant solid fireproof Italian farm houses
on the market in 1970,
scattered across the land.
Sixty thousand affluent foreigners,
to fix them, learn to cook, and write a book.

But in California, houses all are wood—
roads pushed through, sewers dug, lines laid underground—
hundreds of thousands, made of strandboard, sheetrock, plaster.

They won't be here 200 years from now—they'll burn or rot.

No handsome solid second homes for
thousand-year-later wealthy
Melanesian or Eskimo artists and writers here,

—oak and pine will soon return.

from *Catamaran*

Pencil

◇   ◇   ◇

Once, you loved permanence,
Indelible. You'd sink
Your thoughts in a black well,
And called the error, ink.
And then you crossed it out;
You canceled as you went.
But you craved permanence,
And honored the intent.
Perfection was a blot
That could not be undone.
You honored what was not,
And it was legion.
And you were sure, so sure,
But now you cannot stay sure.
You turn the point around
And honor the erasure.
Rubber stubs the page,
The heart, a stiletto of lead,
And all that was black and white
Is in-between instead.
All scratch, all sketch, all note,
All tentative, all tensile
Line that is not broken,
But pauses with the pencil,
And all choice, multiple,
The quiz that gives no quarter,

And Time the other implement
That sharpens and grows shorter.

from *The Atlantic*

ANNE STEVENSON

How Poems Arrive

◇   ◇   ◇

You say them as your undertongue declares
Then let them knock about your upper mind
Until the shape of what they mean appears.

Like love, they're strongest when admitted blind,
Judging by feel, feeling with sharpened sense
While yet their need to be is undefined.

Inaccurate emotion—as intense
As action sponsored by adrenaline—
Feeds on itself, and in its own defense

Fancies its role humanitarian,
But poems, butch or feminine, are vain
And draw their satisfactions from within,

Sporting with vowels, or showing off a chain
Of silver *els* and *ms* to host displays
Of intimacy or blame or joy or pain.

The ways of words are tight and selfish ways,
And each one wants a slot to suit its weight.
Lines needn't scan like this with every phrase,

But something like a pulse must integrate
The noise a poem makes with its invention.
Otherwise, write prose. Or simply wait

Till it arrives and tells you its intention.

from *The Hudson Review*

Substitutions

◊   ◊   ◊

Balsamic, for Zhenjiang vinegar.
Letters, for the family gathered.

A Cuisinart, for many hands.
Petty burglars, for warring bands.

A baby's room, for tight quarters.
Passing cars, for neighbors.

Lawn-mower buzzing, for bicycle bells.
Cod fillets, for carp head-to-tail.

Children who overhear the language,
for children who speak the language.

Virginia ham, for Jinhua ham,
and nothing, for the noodle man,

calling as he bears his pole
down alley and street, its baskets full

of pickled mustard, scallions, spice,
minced pork, and a stove he lights

where the customer happens to be,
the balance of hot, sour, salty, sweet,

which decades later you still crave,
a formula he'll take to the grave.

from *New England Review*

Shooting Wild

◊   ◊   ◊

At the theater I learn *shooting wild*,
a movie term that means filming a scene
without sound, and I think of being a child
watching my mother, how quiet she'd been,

soundless in our house made silent by fear.
At first her gestures were hard to understand,
and her hush when my stepfather was near.
Then one morning, the imprint of his hand

dark on her face, I learned to watch her more:
the way her grip tightened on a fork, night
after night; how a glance held me, the door—
a sign that made the need to hear so slight

I can't recall her voice since she's been dead:
no sound of her, no words she might have said.

from *Poet Lore*

Grief Runs Untamed

◊   ◊   ◊

In one hand the exiles hold a bundle
with a blanket, medicine, and a comb;
in the other, a door handle.
They attach it to every mountain and wall,
hoping the handle will conjure the door
that will open and let them in.

Through the swamps, down the dirt roads,
through the frigid water the exiles go,
knowing they shall never return.
In their former homes, if there are still homes,
the wind wails. Spiders weave
their shrouds over the cupboards and beds.

Cats, left behind, wait to be scratched under their chins;
a dog smells the scarf a young girl dropped
and barks on the cellar stairs.
Near the road thousands took to flee,
a carcass of a cow still tied to the olive tree,
abandoned like their tea sets and pots.

A widow with children runs from the Guatemalan gangs.
Newlyweds from Syria huddle in a dinghy
in the Mediterranean, their wedding rings sold
to help them pay the way. A couple from Sudan
limp along on the scorched ground with their epileptic son.

Those who survive and settle in a new place
sometimes dream at night of returning
by foot to their native homes.
When they wake up, they have blisters on their feet.

from *The Sun*

G. C. WALDREP

Dear Office in Which I Must Account for Tears,

◇ ◇ ◇

You were a forest once. I passed through you
and my garments were torn by thorns.

After that, I did not venture near the lambs
that would be charged with your death.
I did not feed the horses
toward which you were stampeding.

We were young then, together, and then
an art grew up between us.
I received mail at this address long before
my vocation took me here; I discarded it
unopened, a dew upon the stippled grass.

Sometimes I spoke to you, if only in dreams.

Dear Office, the memory of photosynthesis
runs like an electrical current
through your walls, your concrete floors,
the humming bevatron of your dataports.
I have woven new garments
from my own hair, which seeks the earth.

Things I vouchsafe:
I have never been afraid of the falling dream.
I speak in no tongue other than my own.
I cannot even order a meal in your country.

When I sleep at night I recall your secret,
which is the world's secret, only
smaller and green, a lost coin's verdigris.
At those times you are a weather unto me.

Let me be the first to greet you
when you sit at the right hand of our God.

from *Seneca Review*

WANG PING

老家—Lao Jia

◇　◇　◇

At fifteen, my father ran away from his widowed mother to fight the Japanese.

"I'll come back with a Ph.D. and serve my country with better English and
　　knowledge,"
I pledged at the farewell party in Beijing, 1986.

家: *jia*—home: a roof under which animals live.

老家: *lao jia*—old home that ties us to ancestors, land, and sea.

> When asked where I'm from,
> I say "Weihai," even though
> nobody knows where it is,
> even though I've never been to the place.

He lost his left ear in a bayonet fight with a Japanese soldier. Two years later,
American cannons split his eardrums.

The night I arrived at JFK, the Mets won the World Series and the noise on
the street went on till three. I got up at six and went to work in my sponsor's
antique shop in Manhattan.

The bag lady stopped her cart on the busy street and peed onto a subway grate.

"Did you jump or fly?" asked my landlady from her mah-jongg table. Then she
laughed and told me that her husband had jumped ship ten years ago, in Brook-
lyn. When he opened his fifth Chinese take-out, he bought her a passport and
flew her to Queens.

The only thing he liked to talk about was his old home, Weihai, its plump sea cucumbers and sweet apples, men with broad shoulders, stubborn thighs, and girls with long braids making steamed bread.

"I don't know why," she said, shivering behind her fruit stand. "Back home, I could go for days without a penny in my pocket, and I didn't feel poor. Now, if my money goes down below four figures, I panic." She scanned the snow-covered streets of Chinatown. "I guess I really don't want to be homeless here."

I hired the babysitter when she mentioned her hometown—Weihai.

The president visited the rice paddies in Vietnam where a pilot had been downed thirty-three years ago, before he brought his bones back home.

My father tried to return to Weihai after his discharge from the Navy. With his rank, he could find work only in a coal-mine town nearby. My mother refused to go. He went alone, and soon contracted TB. Mother ordered me to date the county administrator's son so my father could come home.

> "No, I'm not sad." The street kid shook her head.
> "How can I miss something I've never had?"

On her sixtieth birthday, my grandma went home to die. She would take two ships, one from the island to Shanghai, then from Shanghai to Yantai. From there, she would take two buses to reach Weihai. I carried her onto the big ship at the Shanghai Port, down to the bottom, where she'd spend three days on a mattress, on the floor, with hundreds of fellow passengers. "How are you going to make it, Grandma?" I asked. She pulled out a pair of embroidered shoes from her parcel and placed them between my feet. "My sweetheart and liver, come to see your old home soon, before it's too late."

House—房—fang: a door over a square, a place, a direction.

He never lost his accent, never learned Mandarin or the island dialect.

Weihai, a small city
in Shandong Province,
on the coast of the Yellow Sea,
a home, where my grandfather
and his father were born,
where my grandma married,
raised her children, and
now lies in the yam fields,
nameless, next to her husband,
an old frontier to fend off Japanese pirates,
a place I come from, have never seen.

Back from America, my mother furnished her home on the island, bought an apartment in a suburb of Shanghai, and is considering a third one in Beijing. "A cunning rabbit needs three holes," she wrote to her daughters, demanding their contributions.

They swore, before boarding the ship, that they'd send money home to bring more relatives over; in return, they were promised that if they died, their bodies would be sent back home for burial.

I drink American milk—a few drops in tea.
I eat American rice—Japanese brand.
Chinese comes to me only in dreams—in black-and-white
      pictures.

Since my father ran away at fifteen, all he talked about was his *lao jia*—old home—on the shore of the Yellow Sea.

Room—屋—*wu*: a body unnamed and homeless until it finds a destination.

We greet a stranger with
"Where are you from?"
When we meet a friend on the street, we say,
"Where have you been? Where are you going?"

My mother buried her husband on the island of East China Sea, where he lived for forty years.

家—a roof under which animals live
房—a door over a square, a place, a direction
屋—a body unnamed and homeless until it finds a destination

—my wandering roots for *lao jia*—老家

from *Poetry*

On a Palm

◇   ◇   ◇

The local psychic closed up shop last week;
Took down her shingle with its big black palm
Held up to lure those driving by away
From busy motions to her inner calm;
To draw them where sharp incense burned and scarves
Billowed mysterious shadows down the hall;
Where faded posters of the astral signs
And chakra nodes sagged from each hapless wall.

She'd greet them in her gold-ringed gypsy getup,
Her hands emerging to enfold their own
And lead them to a table draped in silks
While querying in a warm and foreign tone.
Of late, she'd clutch them with a tighter grip
And seek to stretch one hour into two
With natal charts, then tarot cards, and listening
For any dead who might be passing through.

I'm glad the window's dark, *For Rent* sign hung.
But, when I see my hands gripped round the wheel,
The knuckles growing cracked and lined with age,
I think how there is no one who will peel
Them open, lay the fingers gently straight,
And study all those traceries of fate.

from *Presence*

RYAN WILSON

Face It

◇   ◇   ◇

A silence, bodied like wing-beaten air,
Perturbs your face sometimes when parties end
And, half-drunk, you stand looking at some star
That flickers like a coin wished down a well,
Or when you hear a voice behind you whisper
Your name, and turn around, and no one's there.
You're in it then, once more, the stranger's house
Perched in the mountain woods, the rot-sweet smell
Of fall, the maples' millions, tongues of fire,
And there, whirl harrowing the gap, squint-far,
That unidentified fleck, approaching and
Receding at once, rapt in the wind's spell—
Pulse, throb, winged dark that haunts the clean light's glare—
That thing that you're becoming, that you are.

from *The New Criterion*

CHRISTIAN WIMAN

Assembly

◇ ◇ ◇

It may be Lord our voice is suited now
only for irony, onslaught, and the minor hierarchies of rage.

It may be that only the crudest, cruelest transformations touch us,
gauzewalkers in the hallways of a burn ward.

I remember a blind man miraculous for the sounds of his mouth,
every bird rehearsed and released for the children to cheer.

Where is he now, in what icy facility or sunlit square,
blackout shades and a brambled mouth, singing extinctions?

from *Resistance, Rebellion, Life*

137

CONTRIBUTORS' NOTES AND COMMENTS

ALLISON ADAIR was born in Pittsburgh in 1977 and grew up in Gettysburg and Mechanicsburg, Pennsylvania. She studied at Brown University and the Iowa Writers' Workshop, where she received a Teaching-Writing Fellowship. She teaches at Boston College.

Adair writes: "Though I continued to read and study poetry intensely after graduate school, I didn't write for several years, until one day I had to. During my first pregnancy, I was vacuuming one of two antique Persian rugs, bought online, when suddenly I felt that something was wrong. Something small, wordless. By the following week, the pregnancy had ended. Around that time, moths began to swarm my apartment. I rolled up the edge of the rug I'd been tending to find it threaded through with larvae—they'd been there all along.

"Months later, I was pregnant again. Pregnancy was reconnecting me, physically, to poetry, especially in terms of metaphor: as transfer, and as a paradox wherein the familiar becomes *unfamiliar*, the unfamiliar *familiar*. This strange time is the occasion of 'Miscarriage.' After the second pregnancy ended, I sat down, exhausted, and wrote, from somewhere underneath craft. The poem is decidedly spare—straightforward and bereft. The rug is described literally; the title refuses any play. The only technique I allowed myself, really, comes in the line breaks, which are annotated both in meaning and in sound. But I also couldn't help reflecting on the hands that might have woven that rug, on where the women in the pattern might have existed before arriving in my apartment, on all they'd seen, all their terrible wisdom."

KAVEH AKBAR was born in Tehran, Iran. *Calling a Wolf a Wolf*, his first book, was published in 2017 by Alice James Books in the United States and by Penguin in the United Kingdom. A recipient of a Ruth Lilly and Dorothy Sargent Rosenberg Poetry Fellowship, he teaches at Purdue University and in the low-residency MFA programs at Randolph College and Warren Wilson College.

Of "Against Dying," Akbar writes: "In the summer of 2013, in the throes of one of many rock bottoms, my body began giving up. I was getting sicker and sicker, closer and closer to a Rubicon that, once crossed, could never be crossed back again. One day, grace of graces, I crawled my way toward help and (very) long story short, I slowly began getting better. The poem asks: 'how shall I live now / in the unexpected present?' It was a kind of rebirth. To whom do you submit your gratitude, your bewilderment at being given a second chance? And what to do with a body ravaged by its previous occupant? Roethke said, 'The serious problems in life are never fully solved, but some states can be resolved rhythmically.' This poem is deeply invested in that promise."

JULIA ALVAREZ was born in New York City in 1950, and grew up in her parents' native country of the Dominican Republic. She recently retired as a writer-in-residence at Middlebury College. In addition to poetry, she has written fiction, nonfiction, and books for young readers; titles include: *Homecoming* (Plume, 1996), *The Other Side/El Otro Lado* (Plume, 1996), and *The Woman I Kept to Myself* (A Shannon Ravenel Book, 2011). She received a 2013 National Medal of the Arts and is a founder of Border of Lights, an annual gathering of activists, artists, educators at the border of Haiti and the DR. Visit her at juliaalvarez .com.

Of "American Dreams," Alvarez writes: "When we arrived in New York in 1960, refugees from the dictatorship in the Dominican Republic, my parents kept telling my sisters and me that this was the land of freedom where we had the opportunity to become whatever we wanted to be. They believed in the American Dream. I wish I could say that I shared their high-mindedness. But I was a kid, and my American Dream was all about candy. I couldn't get enough of it. In Queens where we lived there was a whole store dedicated to candy, owned by an immigrant mother and her son, earlier-generation versions of us. I roamed the aisles, pronouncing the alluring names under my breath, the son watching me in a way that unsettled me. (Now, I wonder if he was just worried about shoplifting, not interested in my skinny— despite all that sugar—prepubescent body.) During those early years of my sweets-fixation, Martin Luther King was marching; demonstrators were being attacked by dogs, getting jailed, lynched; girls my age were dying in bombed churches. I'm astonished that those scenes on the news didn't register. Or maybe I was subliminally aware, and that's why I didn't buy the un-nuanced version of the American Dream. The violence on TV was not unlike the violence of the regime we had escaped. The American Dream was not equally accessible to all. The Land of Good and Plenty was still just the name of a candy."

A. R. AMMONS was born outside Whiteville, North Carolina, in 1926. He started writing poetry aboard a US Navy destroyer escort in the South Pacific in World War II. After his discharge, "Archie"—everyone who knew him called him Archie—attended Wake Forest University, where he studied the sciences. He took a class in Spanish, married the teacher, and went on to work as an executive in his father-in-law's biological glass company before he began teaching poetry at Cornell University in 1964. Ammons wrote nearly thirty books of poetry, many published by W. W. Norton, including *Glare* (1997), *Garbage* (1993), *A Coast of Trees* (1981), and *Sphere* (1974). His posthumous books include *Bosh and Flapdoodle* (Norton, 2005), *Selected Poems* (Library of America, 2006), and a two-volume set of his collected poems from Norton in 2017. A longtime and greatly beloved professor at Cornell University, Archie was guest editor of *The Best American Poetry 1994*. He died on February 25, 2001, a week after turning seventy-five.

DAVID BARBER is the author of two collections of poems published by Northwestern University Press: *Wonder Cabinet* (2006) and *The Spirit Level* (1995), which received the Terrence Des Pres Prize from Tri-Quarterly Books. "Sherpa Song" is included in his forthcoming collection, *Secret History*, to be published by Northwestern in 2019. He is the poetry editor of *The Atlantic* and teaches in the Harvard Writing Program.

Of "Sherpa Song," Barber writes: "Mountaineering is known to be a spiritual pursuit and a technical feat. So, too, poems, at least the ones that move mountains. 'Sherpa Song' is one of a series of numbers in my forthcoming collection *Secret History* cast in a stringent nonce form: five stanzas of five lines, all lashed together in a cat's cradle of slant rhymes. The gambit is to grapple with syntax and cadence in tight quarters to get to a vantage point that would otherwise remain out of reach. In this case, hitching my gear to the double-edged cognomen 'sherpa'—both the ancestral and occupational collective term for the storied alpine guides of the Himalayas—was a way of groping toward a rough sympathetic magic that might turn formal stricture into lyric resonance. If pressed on why the form has gotten under my skin, I'd have to echo George Mallory's gnomic rationale for his assaults on Everest: 'Because it's there.' "

ANDREW BERTAINA was born in Merced, California, in 1980. He was raised in Chico, California, and lives in Washington, DC. He works at American University in the library and as an adjunct in the department of literature. His work is available at andrewbertaina.com.

Bertaina writes: "When I wrote 'A Translator's Note,' I had been reading essays about translation, and thinking about the process and about many of the great writers that I've read only in translation. In these essays about translation, particularly with, say, *War and Peace* or *In Search of Lost Time*, I kept reading arguments as to why one translation or another was more artful or precise than what had come before. It seemed, at least to me, that an argument could be made that every book deserved a thousand translations to try and capture all of the nuances of language and thought of the original.

"From there, I thought about the immense amount of importance we attach to meeting a writer, as though in their presence, some of their true essence is distilled, and the residual effects attach themselves to the person witnessing them like dust around stars. With those intertwining notions of translation and authorship in mind, I wrote 'A Translator's Note,' as though merely seeing a writer and the way he bent to talk to a woman somehow superseded the boundaries of language."

FRANK BIDART was born in Bakersfield, California, in 1939. In 1957 he entered the University of California, Riverside. In 1962 he began graduate work at Harvard, where he studied with Reuben Brower and Robert Lowell. His books include *Star Dust* (2005) and *Desire* (1997), both from Farrar, Straus and Giroux. *Desire* received the 1998 Bobbitt Prize from the Library of Congress and the Theodore Roethke Memorial Poetry Prize. *Half-Light: Collected Poems 1965–2016* (FSG) won the Pulitzer Prize and the National Book Award in 2018. Bidart is the coeditor of Robert Lowell's *Collected Poems* (FSG, 2003). He has taught at Wellesley College since 1972. He lives in Cambridge, Massachusetts.

BRUCE BOND was born in Pasadena, California, in 1954 and is the author of twenty books including, most recently, *Immanent Distance: Poetry and the Metaphysics of the Near at Hand* (University of Michigan, 2015), *Black Anthem* (Tampa Review Prize, University of Tampa, 2016), *Gold Bee* (Helen C. Smith Award, Crab Orchard Award, Southern Illinois University Press, 2016), *Sacrum* (Four Way Books, 2017), and *Blackout Starlight: New and Selected Poems 1997–2015* (E. Phillabaum Award, Louisiana State University Press, 2017). Five books are forthcoming: *Rise and Fall of the Lesser Sun Gods* (Elixir Book Prize, Elixir Press, 2018), *Frankenstein's Children* (Lost Horse Press, 2018), *Dear Reader* (Free Verse Editions, 2018), *Words Written Against the Walls of the City* (LSU, 2019), and *Scar* (Etruscan Press, 2020). He is a regents professor of English at the University of North Texas.

Of "Anthem," Bond writes: "This sonnet, as part of a book-length sequence entitled *Black Anthem*, appears in the final section, where the book reflects upon its choices. Why a book of sonnets? Why that form—that intimate space so associated with autonomy and closure—that has, for many, reached the status of the political? Doubtless, it is for this reason, in part, that I wanted to use it, to subvert an ironically rigid reading of form, to illuminate more precisely our relationship to beauty and perception—to music, in particular, whose play of echo and disorder bear associations without becoming identical to them. So odd an age that shed so much light on how language works and does not work seemed so quick to regard the semiotics of certain forms as fixed—not only unrealistic in terms of the way signs work, but also revelatory of a psychology of critical and political engagement. Music, in particular the anthem, seemed a good place to explore this shared psychology, since the anthem resists our projections even as it gives them flesh, and the stakes of musical persuasion can be so high. What I stumbled on, in writing the poem, is how music's resistance can likewise be 'read.' It resonates, not only as the rhetoric that inspires commitment, but also as the extinction of that rhetoric. Music's pulse is made of singular beats, like bodies, lost in time to the equally ephemeral whole. The resistance of form to meaning thus occasions a surprising return to meaning, to a reimagined affirmation and resistance to beauty as a space apart, a veteran's park, a haunted absence at the heart of each, anxious to believe."

GEORGE BRADLEY was born in Roslyn, New York, in 1953 and was educated at Yale University and the University of Virginia. He is the editor of *The Yale Younger Poets Anthology* and the author of five books of verse: one from Yale University Press, three from Knopf, and most recently a volume from Waywiser Press (*A Few of Her Secrets*, 2011). A short story of his was included in the 2010 PEN/O. Henry award anthology. He has worked as a construction foreman, a sommelier, a copywriter, and an editor. Currently, he imports olive oil from a property outside of Florence. He can often be found in Chester, Connecticut.

Of "Those Were the Days," Bradley writes: "The poem chosen for this year's *BAP* depends on a reader's passing familiarity with some of the proverbs and idioms one hears every day, and it progresses—methodically, implacably—by giving each saying a twist. Prior to composition, the idea for the piece floated around in the back of my mind for some time, in part because our culture's old saws so often struck me as at once trenchant and stupid. That is, they contain the wisdom of generations, but it is the conventional wisdom, and while they are food for thought, they are often uttered in lieu of thinking. The more I pondered these sayings, the more they took on ominous overtones. Or perhaps, as I hope the poem suggests, it is the passage of time that alters one's view of such expressions. Contemplating a language is like gazing at stars. You view the past through the lens of the present, and what you see necessarily depends on where you stand."

JOYCE CLEMENT was born in Upstate New York in 1961. In 1986, after a brief stint as a high school English teacher, she moved to central Connecticut where she still lives and works as a sales and marketing systems manager. Her book *Beyond My View* (Endionpress, 2011) received a Haiku Society of America's Merit Book Award. She was also a 2014 Haiku Foundation Touchstone Award winner. Since 2011, she has served as a director of The Haiku Circle, an annual gathering of haiku poets held each June in Northfield, Massachusetts. From 2016 through 2018 she was coeditor of The Haiku Society of America's *Frogpond* journal.

Clement writes: "The haiku sequence 'Birds Punctuate the Days' arose over the course of a year, primarily during writing sessions consisting largely of not-writing. Pen and keyboard were neglected as my thoughts drifted somewhere behind, ahead, and away from me. Then there would occur a sudden flutter of light or startle of sound—a bird moment—that instantly returned me to the present. In this way birds punctuated my days.

"In haiku, the writer is asked to avoid direct metaphor or personification. Instead two images, a fragment and a phrase, are typically placed next to one another, allowing the resulting associations to push, pull, or vibrate between them. Good haiku often offer levels of association, a touch point and then variants that ripple away from the central moment.

"My intent when writing 'Birds' was to present a visual or aural resemblance between bird moment and punctuation mark that would create an immediate and satisfying connection. Beyond that, I wanted to encapsulate the function of the mark through the moment. Beyond that, I wanted to consider the feeling of the mark, to think about how the marks absorb or enhance the essence of what proceeds and follows them. And then, how does the choice of bird species, their known habits and characteristics, shape the feeling and meaning of mark and poem? Then what other natural pauses, shifts in direction, stillnesses, patterns do we encounter in the flow of thought or day that serve as unwritten punctuation? And so on.

"The haiku are small. They leave plenty of white space for a reader to take a breath, contemplate, or let the mind drift . . . and then they punctuate the page again."

BRENDAN CONSTANTINE was born in Los Angeles, California, in 1967. A poet and teacher, Constantine has published four books of poetry: *Letters to Guns* (Red Hen Press, 2009), *Birthday Girl with Possum* (Write Bloody Publishing, 2011), *Calamity Joe* (Red Hen Press, 2012) and *Dementia, My Darling* (Red Hen Press, 2016). He has received grants and commissions from the Getty Museum, James Irvine Foundation, and the National Endowment for the Arts. He teaches creative writing at the Windward School.

Of "The Opposites Game," Constantine writes: "This poem brewed for quite a while. The scenes described actually occurred and were repeated in different classrooms over a few years. I knew I wanted to write about them, but I couldn't make a start, or rather, I tried too hard. It's an old problem: How does one overcome that first (and often shortsighted) understanding of where a poem 'might' end?

"It ultimately came together for a rally held in honor of Gun Violence Awareness Day in Tucson, Arizona. Activist Patricia Maisch, to whom the piece is dedicated, invited me to read at the event. Her name may be familiar in connection to the infamous attack in 2011 at which Representative Gabrielle Giffords was shot along with nineteen others. Six people died, including nine-year-old Christina-Taylor Green. As horrifying a tragedy as it remains, it could've been much worse, for it was Maisch who noticed the shooter trying to reload after he was subdued. She boldly pried bullets from his hand that day and has been protecting her community ever since.

"I knew I would never be able to compose a poem worthy of her spirit. But when a genuine hero asks you to deliver, you tend to focus. I just wanted to make something useful, if only for an afternoon in a public park. I'm very pleased the poem has continued to serve. Patricia seems to like it, too."

MARYANN CORBETT was born in Washington, DC, in 1950, grew up in Northern Virginia, moved to Minnesota in 1972 for graduate school, and has lived in Saint Paul since 1986. She earned a doctorate in English in 1981, specializing in medieval literature and linguistics. For almost thirty-five years she worked as an in-house teacher, editor, and indexer for the Minnesota Legislature, retiring in 2016. She is the author of four books of poetry: *Breath Control* (David Robert Books, 2012), *Credo for the Checkout Line in Winter* (Able Muse, 2013), *Mid Evil*, the winner of the 2014 Richard Wilbur Award (University of Evansville Press, 2015), and *Street View* (Able Muse, 2017).

Of "Prayer Concerning the New, More 'Accurate' Translation of Certain Prayers," Corbett writes: "When the Catholic Church in the United States adopted a new English translation of the Mass a few years ago—a translation that was touted as being more correct and closer to the Latin—many Catholics found the new wording stiff, stilted, and uncomfortable. Many were angry, and I was one of them. Most people gave up being angry, having little choice. But I stayed mad, and one day a couple of years back, this poem bubbled up out of my subconscious, very nearly writing itself."

ROBERT CORDING was born in Englewood, New Jersey, in 1949. He has published eight collections of poems, including *What Binds Us to This World* (Copper Beech Press, 1991), *Heavy Grace* (Alice James, 1996), *Against Consolation* (CavanKerry Press, 2002), *A Word in My Mouth: Selected Spiritual Poems* (Wipf and Stock, 2013), and, most recently, *Only So Far* (CavanKerry, 2015). He taught for thirty-eight years at Holy Cross College in Worcester, Massachusetts. He has received two National Endowment for the Arts fellowships in poetry and two poetry grants from the Connecticut Commission of the Arts.

Of "Toast to My Dead Parents," Cording writes: "This poem began where it ends up: with the idea of a toast. Because a toast is basically honorific and loving, it can also probe and caricature the fault lines of our humanness. A few years after both my parents had died, I was looking for a form that could capture my response to their devoted sixty-three-year marriage, a marriage that also consisted of, from the moment of their rising to the moment they fell asleep, a kind of constant bickering. Despite their basic contentment, something was always not quite right and whatever that something was, it was the other's fault. In the end, the poem turned out to be my own search for whatever it was that lay at the center of their marriage, that made it work and not work, that made their connection both so deep and so unsettling."

Born in Germany in 1968, CYNTHIA CRUZ grew up in Northern California. She is the author of *How the End Begins* (Four Way Books, 2016), *Wunderkammer* (Four Way Books, 2014), *The Glimmering Room* (Four Way Books, 2012), and *Ruin* (Alice James, 2006). Her fifth collection of poems, *Dregs*, will appear from Four Way Books in 2018. She is editing an anthology of Latina poetry, *Other Musics*, which is forthcoming in 2019. She has received a Hodder Fellowship from Princeton University. *Notes Toward a New Language*, a collection of essays on silence and marginalization, is forthcoming in 2018 from BookThug. A doctoral student in German at Rutgers University, she lives in Brooklyn and in Berlin and teaches at Sarah Lawrence College.

Of "Artaud," Cruz writes: "Artaud has been haunting me for most of my life. A ghostly apparition, but always only on the periphery.

"I could never, can never, begin to attempt to articulate how his presence is felt in my life. More importantly, I cannot, have never, been able to articulate Artaud's life. His presence in the world, the many experiences he lived through, the myriad ways he changed the world—there is no way for me to reduce his life. 'Words say little to the mind,' he wrote. Words fail.

"Yet, I wanted to write a poem for Artaud. But how? I knew I could not ventriloquize—how could I ever begin to comprehend what it felt like to live inside his mind and his body? And, at the same time, there was no way I could reduce his life, his presence, to the compression of the form of a poem.

"When students ask me what the difference is between a poem and prose I always tell them the poem's job is to carry that which cannot be said to the reader. If I have something to articulate, I'll write an essay.

"And yet—I couldn't write a poem for Artaud. It felt as if doing so would somehow inflict damage or violence upon him.

"I have been thinking about the archive for the past several years—the act of archiving—lifting memory or images or objects or 'found' text or facts from life and dropping them into the poem—and how by doing so, we might make something more whole. Rather than attempt to describe my life—actually paste real-life evidence into the work. This is how I made the Artaud poem.

" 'Artaud' is a found poem. Its beginning is the list of illustrations included in the text *Antonin Artaud: Selected Writings by Antonin Artaud*. In the same way gathering images from one's life and then pasting them into a poem may relay more about one's life than an attempt to describe one's life through metaphor, the list of illustrations says more about Artaud's life than any attempt at articulation might.

"I revised this original 'found poem' until it seemed finally able to carry the enigmatic and profound weight of the artist's life—all of its beauty and terror, brilliance and sorrow—and that is what you have before you—a kind of archive of his life from childhood to death in which his creativity and passion, his suffering and sadness, remain complex and feral, uncombed, as it were, an X-ray or daguerreotype, of the artist's life."

Dick Davis is professor emeritus of Persian at Ohio State University, where he chaired the department of Near Eastern languages and cultures from 2002 to 2012. He has written scholarly works on both English and Persian literature, as well as eight volumes of his own poetry. His publications, including volumes of poetry and verse translation, have been chosen as books of the year by *The Sunday Times*

(UK, 1989), *The Daily Telegraph* (UK, 1989), *The Economist* (UK, 2002), *The Washington Post* (2010), and *The Times Literary Supplement* (UK, 2013). He has published numerous book-length verse translations from medieval Persian, most recently, *Faces of Love: Hafez and the Poets of Shiraz* (Penguin, 2012), and has been called by *The Times Literary Supplement* "our finest translator from Persian," while *The Washington Post* has referred to him as "our pre-eminent translator from the Persian." His *Love in Another Language: Collected Poems and Selected Translations* was published by Carcanet Press in 2017.

Davis writes: "I'm in my seventies now, and I think many people my age look back on their lives and feel, 'However did all that happen?' 'A Personal Sonnet' is about that feeling, and about what has persisted and stayed with me, often things I could never have imagined when I was young: a tragedy involving my younger brother, my marriage (our honeymoon was in Kerala, India, hence the reference; the sunset was over the bay in Cochin), my long involvement with both English and Persian poetry, my life as a scholar and translator of medieval Persian. One of the things that first attracted me to medieval Persian poetry is that it is highly, almost fetishistically, formal, and my own poems tend to be the same. This poem for me calls up regret, surprise, and great gratitude."

WARREN DECKER was born in the United States in 1977. He has lived in Japan for the last seventeen years and is currently teaching at Momoyama Gakuin University in Osaka.

Decker writes: "Although it may seem paradoxical, my creative process is greatly enhanced by tight restrictions. For 'Today's Special,' my commitment to the rhyme and repetition of the traditional triolet form allowed me to create something that could have never emerged in my prose. I am also convinced that there is a metaphysical power in rhymes. Certain words just long to be together."

SUSAN DE SOLA was born in New York and lives near Amsterdam with her family. She is a past recipient of the David Reid Poetry Translation Prize. She holds a PhD from Johns Hopkins University and is the author of several books on architecture and design. As a photographer, she created the chapbook *Little Blue Man* (Seabiscuit Press, 2013). She is assistant poetry editor for the journal *Able Muse*.

Of "The Wives of the Poets," de Sola writes: "The lines 'All poets' wives have rotten lives / Their husbands look at them like knives' intrigued me, in part because they have led a popular afterlife as a quotation, detached from the fragmentary poem from which they were lifted. The loose 'Doggerel Beneath the Skin' appears in books about Delmore Schwartz in differing versions. I enjoy the idea of a poem in conversation with other poems, and it was intriguing to come across a twentieth-century poem that was both elusive as to its final form, and that gave rise to a quotation that became popular in other contexts, despite its gnomic quality. I suppose I had a desire to tease out its possible meanings, and to give a further perspective on the stock figures of the philandering male poet and his long-suffering wife.

"The poem nearly wrote itself, falling into an anapestic rhythm that seemed to fit with throwing knives, both figuratively 'looking daggers,' and the vaudeville or circuslike atmosphere suggested by the image. The rhythm evoked for me not just the sharp points of knives sailing through the air, but a high-wire trapeze act, a man and a woman swaying dangerously back and forth through the air, just catching or missing each other. Despite its rather neat and controlled form, there was a semi-deliberate decision to break the rhyme scheme in the last stanza. This variation was perhaps an act of closure and of judgment, a handful of daggers landing with finality around their target—but whether it is the male poet or the wife who is skewered in place remains uncertain. The poem's title is right out of the epigraph, but is also a wink at that fount of poetic biography, Samuel Johnson's *Lives of the Poets*."

DANTE DI STEFANO was born in Binghamton, New York, in 1978. He is the author of two poetry collections: *Love Is a Stone Endlessly in Flight* (Brighthorse Books, 2016) and *Ill Angels* (Etruscan Press, forthcoming in 2019). He is the poetry editor for *DIALOGIST*. Along with María Isabel Alvarez, he coedited the anthology *Misrepresented People: Poetic Responses to Trump's America* (NYQ Books, 2018). He teaches high school English in Endicott, New York, and resides in Endwell, New York, with his wife, Christina.

Of "Reading Dostoyevsky at Seventeen," Di Stefano writes: "I'm not sure how I stumbled onto Dostoyevsky, but during my senior year in high school I read *Crime and Punishment*, *Demons* (in a version titled *The Possessed*), *The Idiot*, and *The Brothers Karamazov*. I read them on the bus ride to school, I read them in homeroom, I read them in remedial math class and in AP English, I read them in the lunchroom, I read them at the food pantry where I volunteered every Friday after school, I read them on the bus rides home from soccer games and track meets, I read them at Mass on Sundays, and, every evening, I read them with a flashlight in bed the way seventeen-year-olds today binge-watch Netflix; if I close my eyes, even now, I can still feel the size and shape of the Signet Classic versions that I carried with me constantly like talismans in those days. Reading those novels was the most significant experience of my adolescence, and the defining moment in my education. Dostoyevsky satisfied a hunger for experiences that were unavailable to me in the ramshackle one-horse towns of Upstate New York. Although I didn't write it in high school, my understanding of poetry owes everything to the complex psychological, spiritual, and philosophical architecture of Dostoyevsky's (translated) prose.

"'Reading Dostoyevsky at Seventeen' is itself an exercise in translation. When I reread my poem, I see it as an attempt to convey the atmosphere of those novels and that particular time in my life: the strange bewildering amalgam of desire, wonder, isolation, foolishness, brilliance, holiness, impetuosity, and tempestuousness that one only truly apprehends either in the pages of a Russian novel or in the throes of young adulthood. I've taught high school English for over a decade now, and I try to keep in mind that the loneliness and vulnerability I felt as a teenager are an almost universal condition of that stage in life. My students, most of whom are learning disabled, rarely read more than 140 characters for pleasure, but they are, in their own ways, as voracious for narrative and as fragile as I was at that age. At seventeen, I burned for the fate of Raskolnikov, Stavrogin, Myshkin, Alyosha, Ivan, and, of course, Dmitri. I burned for an impossible sanctified glistening St. Petersburg. As I write this, I am awaiting (any day now) the birth of my first child, a daughter. My wife and our dog are asleep on the couch. It's snowing out. How grateful I am, for the drab suburban streets of Endwell, New York. How grateful I am to David Lehman and Dana Gioia for including my poem in this volume. How grateful I am that, at nearly forty, I burn less like I did at seventeen and more the way G. M. Hopkins's 'fresh-firecoal chestnut-falls.' What I wanted then, but didn't know it, is what I have now, and is also what lit Dostoyevsky's pen: (simple, lambent, clarifying) love."

Nausheen Eusuf is a PhD candidate in English at Boston University, and a graduate of the writing seminars at Johns Hopkins. She is the author of *What Remains* (2011), a chapbook from Longleaf Press, and the full-length collection *Not Elegy, But Eros* (2017), published concurrently by NYQ Books in the United States and Bengal Lights Books in Bangladesh. A native of Bangladesh, she was born in Dhaka, its capital, in 1980.

Of "Pied Beauty," Eusuf writes: "Gerard Manley Hopkins has always been one of my touchstones, so my poem is both response and homage. A meditation on mutability, the poem is about the end of a friend's fifteen-year marriage to a man who proved to be faithless. But in a world tainted by sin, perhaps we must seek aesthetic value in the maculate rather than the immaculate."

JONATHAN GALASSI was born Seattle in 1949. He has published three books of poems, including *Left-Handed* (Knopf, 2012); translations of Italian poets Eugenio Montale, Giacomo Leopardi, and Primo Levi; and a novel about publishers and poets, *Muse* (Knopf, 2015). He lives in New York City, where he works as president and publisher of Farrar, Straus and Giroux.

Galassi writes: "'Orient Epithalamion' is a poem infected with late-season melancholy—one of the most seductive themes there is. It is a love song to the small place where we spend the summer and a marriage song for friends: a wish for their life together, and for the survival of so much that seems in danger of slipping through our fingers as the sweet summer light lessens.

"The poem is a contraption of oppositions, starting from the opening line: 'Fall will touch down in golden Orient.' Autumn decay and disappearance (Keats's ode 'To Autumn' is the hovering locus classicus for this trope) hits up immediately against the trope of recurrence that is contained in the place-name itself, for the sun rises daily, and decay and disappearance are just one act in the endlessly 're-rehearsed' pageant of the seasons. The 'real people' who live here year-round know this, but Orient is also a place of escape, a rural ideal (exemplified in Yeats's 'Lake Isle of Innisfree') for the city folk—the agents, architects, and writers—who come here for refreshment in the green time and see it as one season only. Yet Orient is not a mere idyll; it is a modern place beset by traffic, the vagaries of climate change, and a troubled racial history. This seeming paradise is as potentially fragile as any marriage.

"It's a satire in a Horatian vein, a balladlike still life of characters, flora, fauna, all poised with bated breath at a moment of calm, as the oppositions converge in the resolution of marriage—in this case a very up-to-date same-sex one. A charm against the future, a defiant assertion of what we hope against hope life will be—for Barry and Bill, and for all."

JESSICA GOODFELLOW was born in Salt Lake City in 1965, and grew up outside of Philadelphia. She has graduate degrees from Caltech and the University of New England, in Australia. She currently teaches at a women's college in Kobe, Japan, where she lives with her husband and sons. Her books are *Whiteout* (University of Alaska Press, 2017), *Mendeleev's Mandala* (Mayapple Press, 2015), and *The Insomniac's Weather Report* (Isobar Press, 2014). Recipient of the Chad Walsh Poetry Prize from the *Beloit Poetry Journal* and several awards from the Emrys Foundation, she was a writer-in-residence at Denali National Park and Preserve in the summer of 2016.

Of "Test," Goodfellow writes: "This poem, and all the poems in *Whiteout*, are about my uncle Steve Taylor who, along with six other climbers from the 1967 Wilcox expedition to Denali, died in a terrible and historic ten-day storm having 300-mph winds. My uncle was twenty-two years old. He had lived with our family the previous summer, working and saving money for his senior year at university. I was too young to have any memories from that time. Afterward my grandparents and my mother were stunned into an almost complete silence concerning my uncle and his life. Still, he was a mythic figure in my childhood, perhaps all the more so because of my family's silence. In this poem I wanted to show how grief undealt with is passed along intergenerationally; how profound and long-lasting this secondhand sorrow can be; how it can appear, unbidden, at random moments after many years. Because this poem is also about the SATs, I wanted to use the form of a multiple-choice test, but I found that having only intermittent lines be test questions allowed more narrative flow. I also used in the poem as many words as I could from an official SAT vocabulary list."

SONIA GREENFIELD was born in Peekskill, New York, in 1970. Her book *Boy with a Halo at the Farmer's Market* won the 2014 Codhill Poetry Prize. Her chapbook, *American Parable*, won the 2017 Autumn House Press/Coal Hill Review Prize and was published in 2018. She lives with her husband and son in Hollywood where she edits the *Rise Up Review* and codirects the Southern California Poetry Festival.

Greenfield writes: "When I read of the 'Ghost Ship' fire in Oakland at the artists' warehouse, and I read of the individuals who were lost in the fire, I realized how much those people were like me twenty years ago trying to make it in the Bay Area, trying to figure out my sexuality and in love with the creativity and drama of being young in the city. Besides the years between us—the then and now—the only thing that separates them from me is chance: my luck and their misfortune. My warehouse, their warehouse. It's a terrible story and too true in terms of how fate works. We can let that freeze us or we can let that free us. In between those distinctions, we grieve."

JOY HARJO was born in Tulsa, Oklahoma, in 1951. *Conflict Resolution for Holy Beings* (W. W. Norton, 2015), her most recent book of poetry, was shortlisted for the international Griffin Prize. She was recently awarded the Ruth Lilly Prize from the Poetry Foundation. She is at work on a new poetry collection, a historical memoir, and a musical play, *We Were There When Jazz Was Invented* (for which she is writing the book of the play and the music). She is the founder of For Girls Becoming, a mentorship program in the arts for Mvskoke tribal young women, and holds the John C. Hodges Chair of Excellence at the University of Tennessee, Knoxville.

Of "An American Sunrise" Harjo writes: "The poem is a Golden Shovel, a form concocted by Terrance Hayes in which he borrowed a line from a Gwendolyn Brooks poem and used each word as an end line. You can use this form with any poem. I went traditional and used a line from Brooks's 'We Real Cool' to form the end words and went from there. The end words gave the poem a momentum. I could barely keep up. Brooks is still a teacher, always will be. And in pool halls and bars will always be found the dancers, dreamers, and visionaries. It's a tough road here in this country of Natives, immigrants, and refugees, and many get lost. History is a layered dynamic force carried forth in our songs, poems, and stories. We are many voices and will never be captured in the voice of a single authoritarian speaker who hard lines the ideal."

TERRANCE HAYES was born in Columbia, South Carolina, in 1971. He is the author, most recently, of *American Sonnets for My Past and Future*

Assassin (Penguin, 2018). His other books are *How to Be Drawn* (Penguin, 2015), *Lighthead* (Penguin, 2010), *Wind in a Box* (Penguin, 2006), *Hip Logic* (Penguin, 2002), and *Muscular Music* (Tia Chucha Press, 1999). He won the National Book Award in 2010 and a MacArthur Fellowship in 2014. He served as the guest editor of *The Best American Poetry 2014*.

Of "American Sonnet for My Past and Future Assassin," Hayes writes: "Love poems, like love, can/should transmit a few mixed messages and unanswerable questions."

ERNEST HILBERT was born in Philadelphia in 1970. He is the author of three collections of poetry, *Sixty Sonnets* (Red Hen Press, 2009), *All of You on the Good Earth* (Red Hen Press, 2013), and *Caligulan* (Measure Press, 2015), which was selected as winner of the 2017 Poets' Prize. He lives in Philadelphia where he works as a rare book dealer, opera librettist, and literary journalist. He writes about books for *The Washington Post*.

Hilbert writes: "I encountered *Mars Ultor* on a visit to the palatial Getty Villa. There I stood, confronted by this robust, warlike figure, his muscles coiled, his powerful right arm held up in triumph—a provocative sight, yet only four inches tall: small enough to slip into my pocket, a lararium statuette, which is to say a household god. Here was the mighty and vengeful warrior god on the scale of a Hummel figurine, a portable deity, suitable for a shelf or for travel on campaign with a legionary; a symbol of confidence, conquest, success, domination; a charm for winners. Despite his daunting moniker, he is easy to miss amid the museum's more than forty thousand ancient Mediterranean artifacts.

"I drew out my notebook. He had me thinking about power, how it underpins any republic or empire, ordered or chaotic, and is felt most acutely in times when power is transferred, a process that can be orderly but is more often than not tumultuous in some regard, even in democratic civilizations. It brought to mind unsettling notions I first encountered long ago when I read James George Frazer's *The Golden Bough*. The aging king must be strangled upon his throne in order for a proper exchange of power to occur.

"The term *virtù* appears in the poem. Niccolò Machiavelli used it to describe the potency and force of a leader. The word summons qualities of civic pride but also some amount of ruthlessness. Is *virtù* virtue?

We take solace in the rule of law, believing no one is above it, understanding that it is a transcendent organizing principle used to correct dangerous political aberrations. Yet history has shown that law without the final threat of force behind it can all too often prove toothless. The treaties I invoke are like those high-minded and cunning documents that bound the capitals of Europe (many of them secret) in the years of 'The Great Game' while hastening the suicidal Great War that enveloped the continent. The poem considers such devices used to constrain, redirect, or, at times, cloak pure power and allow societies to function.

"'Mars Ultor' first appeared in a sober, high-circulation journal called *Academic Questions*, a publication of the National Association of Scholars. Not long after, with the election of Donald Trump, the poem took on a second life. It was enlisted by publisher Henry Wessells for the pages of his protest magazine *Donald Trump: The Magazine of Poetry*, issued in the spirit of *Ronald Reagan: The Magazine of Poetry*. Following Trump's inauguration, protesters at Trump Tower took to reading my poem aloud in the lobby. In the long view that informs 'Mars Ultor,' a blustering giant may one day be deemed harmless, another lararium statuette reduced in size from a colossal temple god."

R. NEMO HILL was born on Long Island, New York, in 1955. He attended college for one semester, but quickly dropped out. After a brief stint as a baker, he plunged almost immediately into travel and various entrepreneurial endeavors—including a greeting card company, a Balinese import company, and (at present) an indigo dyeing operation. He has lived in New York City, San Francisco, and Portugal, and has traveled extensively in Southeast Asia. All along the way he has been writing. He is the author, in collaboration with painter Jeanne Hedstrom, of an illustrated novel, organized around the processes of Medieval alchemy, *Pilgrim's Feather* (Quantuck Lane Press, 2002); a narrative poem based upon a short story by H. P. Lovecraft, *The Strange Music of Erich Zann* (Hippocampus Press, 2004); a chapbook in heroic couplets, *Prolegomena to an Essay on Satire* (Modern Metrics/EXOT BOOKS, 2006); and two collections of poems, *When Men Bow Down* (Dos Madres Press, 2012) and *In No Man's Ear* (Dos Madres, 2016). Forthcoming is a book of *ghazals*, *Magellan's Reveries*. He is also editor and publisher of EXOT BOOKS, www.exot.typepad.com/exotbooks.

Hill writes: "'The View from The Bar' is an elegy for a very real place in New York City, a gay dive bar known as The Bar, which was located on the corner of 4th Street and 2nd Avenue. True dive bars are, unfortunately, an endangered species in the newly sanitized New York, and though this one still exists, I wonder how much longer it can hold on. It was a seminal place for me for decades, and living in a tiny tenement apartment in the East Village for thirty-five years it became my home away from home. Many of my drinking companions from those days have died, and others have drifted away less dramatically. A fire devastated The Bar, and its name has changed twice since then, along with its clientele. I have fled the city myself now, alarmed by the arguably brutal changes in my old neighborhood. But I can no sooner forget those many intimate nights in The Bar than I can forget the murky, low-rent Camelot of my own youth."

Tony Hoagland (b. 1953) teaches at the University of Houston and elsewhere. He has published eight books, including most recently the poetry collections *Recent Changes in the Vernacular* (Tres Chicas Books, 2018) and *Priest Turned Therapist Treats Fear of God* (Graywolf Press, 2018).

Hoagland writes: "I wrote the best lines of 'Into the Mystery' as part of a birthday poem for a friend whose house we were going to for dinner one night. We ate at a picnic table in the backyard, with candles and Christmas lights on strings on a perfect summer night in New Mexico. It was a nice evening, and I read the poem out loud, but my friend didn't seem especially impressed and so I put it away in a drawer, thinking it not very good. But the best lines seemed true to me and I pulled them out a year later in another place and transplanted them to a different, more enclosed backyard garden, in Houston, a place where I would often sit by myself in the dark and recover from city life. The poem became imaginatively reassigned to my friend Lillie Robertson, whom I imagined coming there to sit in her own solitary reverie. The second poem is much shorter, more lyrical, and its mostly endstopped couplets are meant to evoke the state of wonder, and arrival, suitable for a soul that has had the character to endure."

Anna Maria Hong's first poetry collection, *Age of Glass*, won the Cleveland State University Poetry Center's 2017 First Book Poetry Competition and was published in the spring of 2018. Her novella,

H & G, won the A Room of Her Own Foundation's inaugural Clarissa Dalloway Prize and was published by Sidebrow Books in early 2018. Her second poetry collection, *Fablesque*, won Tupelo Press's Berkshire Prize and is forthcoming in 2019. A former Bunting Fellow at the Radcliffe Institute for Advanced Study, she has joined the literature faculty at Bennington College.

Hong writes: "I drafted 'Yonder, a Rental' toward the end of my seven-year run of writing sonnets, a project that yielded more than three hundred poems, which I winnowed down to the sixty-four sonnets that constitute *Age of Glass*. In composing this poem, I eschewed the familiar English and Italian rhyme schemes that I'd inhabited in previous sonnets, working instead with pairs of rhymes that appear throughout the lines to create a kind of double helix of sound.

"The figure of the moon and the event of collapsed empire that animate this poem also recur throughout *Age of Glass*. I chose the antiquated word 'Oriental' to exploit its Eurocentric associations with otherness."

PAUL HOOVER was born in Harrisonburg, Virginia, in 1946, in the Shenandoah Valley, and raised in the rural Midwest. He is now professor and acting chair of the creative writing department of San Francisco State University. Following the departure of coeditor Maxine Chernoff, he serves as sole editor of the literary annual *New American Writing*. His fifteen books of poetry include *The Book of Unnamed Things* (Plume Editions/MadHat Press, 2018), *Desolation: Souvenir* (Omnidawn Publishing, 2012), and *In Idiom and Earth/En el idioma y en la tierra*, a selection of poems, 2002–2006, translated by María Baranda (Mexico City: Conaculta Práctica Mortal, 2012). His translation with Baranda of the complete *Poesías* of San Juan de la Cruz will be published in late 2018 by Milkweed Editions.

Hoover writes: "The phrase 'I am the size of what I see' appears in Fernando Pessoa's *The Book of Disquiet*, translated by Richard Zenith. I took the book with me on a trip to Barcelona, because I was traveling alone and knew that, for all its existential rawness, it would make good company. In my early seventies, I am now a man 'of a certain age,' as they say, and since I began writing poetry I've had the feeling of arriving late. I can speak as quietly as any leaf and expect to depart unnoticed, 'not even a smudge on the glass.' I didn't plan to write on that theme. It seemed to arrive with the pronoun 'I.' I'm fascinated, too, by the relativity of youth and age. How much of the water we drink is new and how much is ancient? Both young and old eyes can see that the match flaming in one's fingers is the size of a tree in the distance. It's that kind of natural magic/metaphysics that interests me as a poet."

MARIE HOWE is the author of four poetry collections, the most recent of which is *Magdalene* (W. W. Norton, 2017). She lives in New York City and teaches at Sarah Lawrence College.

Of "Walking Home," Howe writes: "The last time I walked out of my mother's home I took a piece of the jigsaw puzzle she'd been working with on the card table. I took some of the sky—my mother had just died—and later put it in a frame, and hung it on my studio wall.

"Life collects into such moments: walking with a daughter, the give and gab of it, the easy talk, walking the round of errands in New York City. The actual—when framed—assumes a completeness, although it is a piece of something so much larger.

"Is it the frame that makes it seem so?"

MANDY KAHN (b. 1978) is the author of two poetry collections, *Glenn Gould's Chair* (2017) and *Math, Heaven, Time* (2014), both from London-based Eyewear Publishing. She frequently collaborates with composers to create works that combine poetry with classical music and was a librettist for MacArthur fellow Yuval Sharon's mobile opera *Hopscotch*. She lives where she was born: in Los Angeles.

Of "Ives," Kahn writes: "In the 1890s, when he was a college student, composer Charles Ives was writing music that was astoundingly complex for its time—music that was polytonal and polyrhythmic, that featured quarter tones and tone clusters—and he was disappointed that others considered it strange. Soon after graduating, Ives declared he did not intend to 'starve on dissonances' and took a job selling insurance. He continued to compose, privately and quietly, after-hours. Two decades passed this way. When a heart attack made Ives fear his life might be nearing its end, he self-published his music and sent it to a group of working conductors. Only then did his public career begin.

"The poem 'Ives' appears in my collection *Glenn Gould's Chair*, a book that weaves snippets from the lives of composers into a larger consideration of the creative life. While researching the book, I began to think of the comfort or discomfort each composer experienced surrounding the great privilege, the great burden of bearing their gifts as forming a kind of spectrum, with Claude Debussy on the far left, the extreme of discomfort, and beside him, Mozart, whose life was also plagued by wild frustration—and with Philip Glass, whose peacefulness astounds me, sitting furthest to the right. I'd often think of Debussy's and Mozart's desperate letters to patrons or friends, begging for commissions or loans or understanding, and then I'd think of Glass's daily routine—meditation, writing, food, meditation, all suffused by a gentle but powerful calm. And then there was Ives, seated nearest to Glass, with his life's output squirreled away in drawers, ready to be shared or not shared, enriching him just by having stepped forth, just by being. And I'd wonder, Do we choose how comfortably we live as what we are, or do our propensities choose for us? Did Ives choose? Does Glass? Did Mozart? Do I? Or: How can I choose better? How can I more fully welcome peacefulness into the body—peacefulness through practice, peacefulness through allowing? And: To honor our gifts fully, must we share them? Or is it enough for them to enrich us, unshared? Can we ourselves, and privately, love the bird, the work—or is it only a bird when it has flown?"

ILYA KAMINSKY was born in Odessa, Ukraine, in 1977, and currently lives in San Diego. His books include *Dancing in Odessa* (Tupelo Press, 2004) and *Deaf Republic* (forthcoming from Graywolf Press in 2019). He is the coeditor of *The Ecco Anthology of International Poetry* (HarperCollins, 2010) and other books.

Of "We Lived Happily During the War," Kaminsky writes: "This poem is a response to George W. Bush's wars. I was visiting the poet Eleanor Wilner at the time. The poem is dedicated to her. I tend to keep poems in a drawer for several years before they get published. Unfortunately, this piece seems just as timely now as when it was written; I wish it was otherwise."

STEPHEN KAMPA was born in Missoula, Montana, in 1981 and grew up in Daytona Beach, Florida. Educated at Carleton College and Johns Hopkins University, he is the author of three collections of poetry:

Cracks in the Invisible (Ohio University Press, 2011), *Bachelor Pad* (Waywiser, 2014), and *Articulate as Rain* (Waywiser, 2018). He teaches at Flagler College in Saint Augustine, Florida, and from time to time works as a musician.

Of "The Quiet Boy," Kampa writes: "Sometimes, to break the ice, I ask my students what superpower they would choose if they could choose any. This often ends up seeming like a one-question personality test. Lots of kids want to fly. Some want to be super-strong or -fast. I caution them about time travel: it just messes everything up, and besides—as Albert Goldbarth has reminded us in more than one poem—we are all already traveling through time anyway. At least one of them argued for immortality as a superpower, and who could fault him for that? But the students that break my heart are the ones who choose invisibility. Faced with a question about power, they pick the only option that is literally self-effacing.

"Surely it must seem that I wrote this poem in response to that response, but the truth of the matter is that the poem preceded the question: I only started asking my students what superpower they might want after I had finished the poem, which began in woolgathering during a cross-country drive. Although I wish I could say 'The Quiet Boy' arose out of compassion for my students' unintentional vulnerability, it didn't. Then again, poems aren't always about responses. Sometimes they're about what questions we should be asking."

Donika Kelly was born in Los Angeles, California, in 1983. She is the author of the chapbook *Aviarium* (500 Places, 2017), and the full-length collection *Bestiary* (Graywolf Press, 2016), winner of the 2015 Cave Canem Poetry Prize and the 2017 Hurston/Wright Award for poetry. A Cave Canem Graduate Fellow, she received her MFA in Writing from the Michener Center for Writers and a PhD in English from Vanderbilt University.

Of "Love Poem: Chimera," Kelly writes: "The chimera I'm thinking of in the poem is the one with a lion's body and a serpent for the tail. That part of the configuration makes sense to me in an associative way. But there's also a goat's head placed, inexplicably, in the middle of the lion's back. Part of what sparked the poem was my confusion at that placement, and I wanted to think about its genesis and birth, and what it might mean to find a family within oneself."

SUJI KWOCK KIM's parents and grandparents were all born in what is now North Korea, where her grandfather, uncle, aunt, and cousins still live. She is the author of *Notes from the Divided Country* (Louisiana State University Press, 2003), which won the Addison Metcalf Award from the American Academy of Arts and Letters (selected by Charles Simic), the Walt Whitman Award from the Academy of American Poets (selected by Yusef Komunyakaa), and the Northern California Book Award/Bay Area Book Reviewers Award; *Private Property*, a multimedia play performed at the Edinburgh Festival Fringe; and *Disorient*, which is forthcoming. Her work has been performed by the Tokyo Philharmonic Chorus, recorded for the Canadian Broadcasting Corporation and National Public Radio, and translated into Russian, German, Spanish, Italian, Croatian, Korean, Japanese, Bengali, and Arabic.

Kim writes: " 'Sono' is dedicated to my son, when he was 'not yet alive but not not,' 'scudding wave after wave of what-might-never-have-been.' The poem's working title, for several drafts, and several miscarriages, had been 'Fugue,' from the Latin, *fuga*, related to both *fugare* ('to chase') and *fugere* ('to flee'). Thankfully, things changed.

"Special thanks to both editors: Dana Gioia, on the American side of the Atlantic, and Patrick Cotter, in Ireland, without whom this poem would not be in print here now."

KARL KIRCHWEY was born in Boston in 1956 and has lived in the United States, the United Kingdom, Switzerland, and Italy. He is the author of seven books of poetry, including most recently *Stumbling Blocks: Roman Poems* (TriQuarterly/Northwestern, 2017). He has translated Paul Verlaine's first book as *Poems Under Saturn* (Princeton University Press, 2011), and is currently working on a first *Selected Poems* in English by Italian poet Giovanni Giudici (1924–2011). He also edited the Everyman's Library Pocket Poets volume *Poems of Rome* (Everyman's Library, 2018). For many years director of the Poetry Center of the 92nd Street Y in New York, Kirchwey has taught in the creative writing program at Bryn Mawr College and served as Andrew Heiskell Arts Director at the American Academy in Rome. He is professor of English and creative writing at Boston University, where he is associate dean of faculty for the humanities.

Kirchwey writes: " 'Palazzo Maldura' refers to the building housing the Department of Language Studies and Literature at the University of Padua (Italy), and is a meditation on my own relationship to books and to learning, as well as on the nonchalant grace with which ancient Italian buildings sometimes accommodate modern functions. The poem acknowledges several poetic predecessors: 'book-worming' is borrowed from Robert Lowell; the 'nymphs and satyrs' might also figure on Keats's Grecian urn; and the 'local habitation' originates with Theseus in *A Midsummer Night's Dream*. (It was also part of the stated mission of Dr. William Kolodney, when he founded The Poetry Center of the 92nd Street YM-YWHA in 1939, to provide for poetry 'a local habitation and a name.') But the spirit of the poem is really that articulated by Chaucer when he wrote, 'The lyf so short, the craft so longe to lerne': there is an infinite amount for a poet to know. My own literary education encouraged a deep humility, when confronted with this infinity. And the only permanent thing, perhaps, is the curiosity that keeps someone tracking an idea from one book to another on the library shelves. This can be a solitary pastime, but it is also a deeply exciting one. The speaker of the poem turns the corner in the stacks, thinking he recognizes another seeker: but it is only his own reflection, since the risk of solipsism, for a writer, is always present. And the mirrored wall also suggests that the search cannot be an indefinite one, since it is limited by a human lifetime."

NATE KLUG was born in Minneapolis in 1985. He is the author of *Rude Woods*, a modern translation of Virgil's *Eclogues* (The Song Cave, 2013), and *Anyone*, a book of poems (University of Chicago Press, 2015). He works as a Protestant minister and lives in Albany, California.

Klug writes: " 'Aconite' began in the experience of reading, as I discovered these amazing names (wolfsbane, monkshood, devil's helmet) for a flower I thought I had seen recently on a walk. Once I found out that this plant (which looked to me like a buttercup) could poison human beings but nourish smaller creatures such as moths, I was hooked. The poem unspooled as I played with names and sounds.

"At some point, with the help of the internet, I stumbled upon Pliny's and Ovid's different discussions of the flower. They each speculate on aconite's etymology and hardscrabble origins (*a-conite*, 'without dust'). As one story goes, Cerebrus, the three-headed dog who guarded Hades, was dragged from the Underworld by Hercules. While the dog struggled in the unfriendly daylight, he 'spit his slavering froth / Upon the greenish grasse. This froth (as men suppose) took roote /

And thriving in the battling soyle in burgeons forth did shoote, / To bane and mischief men withall' (Ovid, tr. Arthur Golding).

"Spit and blossom, sustenance and toxin—commixed in the language itself. As I wrote, I remembered that the flower I'd seen on the trail was white, not the more common purple-blue of aconite (though aconite can also be white). So it may be that I misidentified the plant in the first place. Where do our stories come from? How much does it matter that they are true, and why does truth seem to waver in our telling?"

Robin Coste Lewis is the poet laureate for the city of Los Angeles, a Writer-in-Residence at the University of Southern California, and an Art of Change fellow at the Ford Foundation. She was born in Compton, California, and her family is from New Orleans. She is the author of *Voyage of the Sable Venus* (Knopf, 2015), winner of the National Book Award for poetry—and the first poetry debut to win the award in many years. With Kevin Young, she has written a series of commissioned poems that accompany Robert Rauschenberg's drawings in *Thirty-Four Illustrations for Dante's Inferno* (MoMA, 2017).

Of "Using Black to Paint Light," Lewis writes: "The Metropolitan Museum of Art's recent exhibition on Matisse's creative process, for me, was an interrogation of the aesthetic uses of obsession. For me, the exhibition re-framed intense desire as a gift rather than a burden. Matisse would paint or sketch the same subject over and over and over again. It felt like the best kind of love to me. At the time that I wrote this poem, I was working on a large project regarding Arctic explorer Matthew Henson. I was obsessed with Henson's biography and his location in history. Like Matisse, I was writing poems about Henson over and over and over again. I was particularly obsessed with Henson's passion to reach the North Pole as a black man, to gain further honor for African Americans—an elegant black passion that remains on some historical academic shelf called institutional racism. So many under-investigated narratives still linger there, including the history of the Arctic. And so walking through this Matisse exhibit, I had Henson very much on my mind. But more than that, I had obsession on my mind. Matisse, Henson, and I formed a love triangle, and what we had/have in common, what their lives continue to teach me is that passion, as an aesthetic tool, is the liberator."

DAVID MASON was born in Bellingham, Washington, in 1954 and now teaches at Colorado College. He served as Colorado poet laureate from 2010 to 2014. Among his many books are *The Country I Remember* (Story Line Press, 1996), *Ludlow: A Verse Novel* (Red Hen Press, 2007; 2nd ed., 2010), *The Sound: New and Selected Poems* (Red Hen Press, 2018), and *Voices, Places: Essays* (Paul Dry Books, 2018). He wrote the libretti for Lori Laitman's opera of *The Scarlet Letter* and Tom Cipullo's *After Life*, both of which are available on CD from Naxos. Mason divides his time between the United States and Australia.

Of "First Christmas in the Village," Mason writes: "Some of my favorite poems about religion—Cavafy's 'Myris: Alexandria, A.D. 340' and Eliot's 'Journey of the Magi' spring to mind—see it from outside the circle of belief. In such poems, the mysteries of birth and death are both literal and figurative, like moments of changing consciousness. There is a true story behind this poem, set in Greece in 1980, in a village where superstition and custom still exerted atavistic power. Fire really was carried in a bucket from one hearth to another. Sleep really was like a grave with the covering stone rolled away."

ROBERT MORGAN was born in Hendersonville, North Carolina, in 1944, and grew up on the nearby family farm. He has published fifteen volumes of poetry, most recently *Terroir* (Penguin, 2011), and *Dark Energy* (Penguin, 2015). He is the author of ten works of fiction including *Chasing the North Star* (Algonquin Books, 2016) and three books of nonfiction including *Lions of the West* (Algonquin Books, 2011). He has taught since 1971 at Cornell University, where he is Kappa Alpha Professor of English.

Morgan writes: " 'Window' was inspired by a walk in the woods of Upstate New York in late fall when most of the trees were bare, except for one oak that still had leaves of orange, lavender, and silver. The colors were so striking I thought of a stained glass window over an altar, in the dark woods, with the scent of rotting leaves and mulch all around. We never know when and where we may encounter the sacramental."

AIMEE NEZHUKUMATATHIL was born in Chicago, Illinois, in 1974. She is the author of four books of poetry, including *Oceanic* (Copper Canyon Press, 2018); *Lucky Fish* (2011), winner of the Independent

Publisher Book Awards gold medal in poetry; *At the Drive-In Volcano* (2007), winner of the Balcones Prize, and *Miracle Fruit* (2003), winner of the *ForeWord Magazine* Poetry Book of the Year, the last of which are from Tupelo Press. With Ross Gay, she is coauthor of the chapbook *Lace & Pyrite: Letters from Two Gardens* (Organic Weapon Arts Press, 2014). A collection of nature essays is forthcoming from Milkweed Editions. She is poetry editor of *Orion* magazine and has served as faculty for the Kundiman Retreat for Asian American writers. She is professor of English and creative writing in the MFA program at the University of Mississippi.

Of "Invitation," Nezhukumatathil writes: "The poem started out as one of the only direct addresses to the reader in my most recent collection and it was the first time I had ever used the word 'oceanic' in a poem. In revision, I found myself imagining not only the reader, but my husband (before *and* after our marriage), our children, my students, beloved friends, and perhaps even that stranger who thinks she won't like to read poems. I originally intended it as an *ars poetica*, a poem about the act of writing poetry, but now I also see it as a kind of manifesto—in fact, this poem might be a gentle dare for all of us to make joyful note of outdoor wonderments before they disappear entirely from this planet. I'm gratefully reminded of Toi Derricotte's speech at the National Book Awards where she asserted, 'Joy is an act of resistance.' "

HIEU MINH NGUYEN was born in 1991, the son of Vietnamese immigrants. His debut collection of poetry, *This Way to the Sugar*, appeared from Write Bloody Publishing in 2014; *Not Here* was released by Coffee House Press in 2018. He has received awards and fellowships from the National Endowment for the Arts, Kundiman, the Vermont Studio Center, the Minnesota State Arts Board, and the Loft Literary Center. He attends the MFA Program for Writers at Warren Wilson College. He lives in Minneapolis.

Of "B.F.F.," Nguyen writes: "I cannot talk about this poem without first talking about my favorite movies: Kirsten Dunst washes a car in San Diego, Molly Ringwald applies lipstick (*no hands! no hands!*), Kate Hudson on Quaaludes, Julia Stiles covered in paint, Rachael Leigh Cook covered in paint—am I making any sense? I really really hope so. For most of my life, it seemed impossible to want the things I wanted. I thought, if I couldn't have it—the boy outside my window, the surprise serenade in the bleachers—I could, at least, be in proximity to it. If I couldn't be deemed beautiful, I could stand next to beautiful things."

ALFRED NICOL was born in 1956 in Amesbury, Massachusetts, where he attended the French-Canadian parochial school in which his parents both began and ended their education. He found a mentor in Sydney Lea at Dartmouth College, and another in Rhina Espaillat of the Powow River Poets of Newburyport, Massachusetts, where he lives with his wife Gina DiGiovanni. Nicol is the author of three books of poetry: *Animal Psalms* (Able Muse Press, 2016), *Elegy for Everyone* (Prospero's World Press, 2009), and *Winter Light* (University of Evansville Press, 2004), which received the 2004 Richard Wilbur Award.

Nicol writes: "My poem 'Addendum' riffs on a survival method that Jesus—among the greatest of didactic poets—recommended to his first-century friends: 'Give to Caesar what belongs to Caesar and give to God what belongs to God.' That would still seem the best way for a twenty-first-century poet to balance the demands of the world with the demands of his art, but there's a lot of pressure from the Caesar side to increase its share. I'm old-fashioned enough to consider poetry—and any art that results from inspiration—as stuff to which Caesar should have no claim. But my poem takes the ironic position that, things being what they are, *everything* should go to Caesar."

NKOSI NKULULEKO, a musician and writer, was born in Harlem, New York, in 1996. He has received fellowships from Poets House, the Watering Hole, and *Callaloo*. He is the author of the chapbooks *American/Unknown* (Penmanship Books, 2016) and *Bone Discography* (self-published, 2016). He has performed for TEDxNewYork and the Aspen Ideas Festival. He would like to give a shout out to Harlem.

Nkululeko writes: "'Skin Deep' attempts to bridge intimate duties with the consequences of the external world. At a young age, many are taught concepts of contribution in the home, the importance of sustaining the family's society, but in the poem, I dive into questions of what it means for the society of a country to betray you and the vision of blackness. To clean and be cleaned, these are the physical actions I wished to show in order to highlight the horrors; how one sees the self, how the world (or more specifically, those who seek to control and torment it) distorts identity. The line in which 'the / spoon bends' refers to a scene in *The Matrix*. How much has our reality been stained? What other simple duties do we adhere to that are, in fact, in the service of blurring truths?"

SHEANA OCHOA is a second-generation Mexican American born in Pomona, California, in 1971. Her book, *Stella! Mother of Modern Acting* (Applause Theatre & Cinema, 2014) is the first biography of acting legend Stella Adler. Ochoa, who works as a cultural critic, is writing a historical novel set against the backdrop of the Ludlow Massacre. You can find her most days on Twitter @SheanaOchoa.

Of "Hands," Ochoa writes: "A poem's ability to reflect the temporal, ever-changing mind-set of the reader is miraculous. Stop and think about how many times you've returned to a favorite poem and how each time it revealed something new to you according to your state of mind. As I reread my own poem, it has little resemblance in meaning to the poem I first put down on paper. Today, it is less homage to my lineage than wonder at the elusive nature of identity. Today, I find myself reinventing who I am, conscious that whatever I come up with will simply be another story I am telling myself, another narrative that can at any time be altered, lost, denied, or affirmed. Even the mole on my hand, which is real, has changed. It is no longer flat and brown, but raised and white like a wart. What does this say about the mysteries hidden there? And how my body, which I merely thought of as a machine if I thought of it at all when I originally wrote 'Hands,' has become the gateway to a deeper, more fulfilling understanding of who I am? It becomes palpable how, like human beings, poetry is alive, just waiting for you to come and look into its shifting mirror again."

SHARON OLDS was born in San Francisco, California, in 1942. Her most recent collection of poems, *Odes*, was published by Knopf in 2016; her other books include *The Dead and the Living* (Knopf, 1984), which received the National Book Critics Circle Award, and *Stag's Leap* (Knopf, 2012), which won both the T. S. Eliot Prize and the Pulitzer Prize. She teaches in the graduate creative writing program at New York University, and was a founder, in 1986, of the Goldwater Hospital Writing Workshops. She was New York State Poet from 1998 to 2000.

Olds writes: "'Silver Spoon Ode' was one of the odes that came along during the year or two after my book *Odes* was published. It was written, I think, in June 2016, in the Sierra Nevada, at the writing conference I've been going to for something like thirty years. Each morning, each poet there, including the staff poets, brings a new first draft, or fragment, or *something* new, to one of the five tables with one of the five staff poets as part of the circle. We don't suggest revisions, but try to describe what we see as the strengths of the piece.

"The first line, I remember, first occurred halfway through another poem—then I had the idea (the idea had me) that it might have a poem of its own. And this was a gathering of writers wanting to push ourselves beyond our usual limits—which helped me notice my complaining and bragging. And that noticing called up Lucille—wise woman, wild woman—and the poem was handed to her, and she finished it for me."

JACQUELINE OSHEROW was born in Philadelphia, Pennsylvania, in 1956. She is the author of seven collections of poetry: *Looking for Angels in New York* (University of Georgia Press, 1988), *Conversations with Survivors* (Georgia, 1994), *With a Moon in Transit* (Grove Press, 1996), *Dead Men's Praise* (Grove, 1999), *The Hoopoe's Crown* (BOA Editions, 2005), *Whitethorn* (Louisiana State University Press, 2011) and *Ultimatum from Paradise* (LSU, 2014). She has received grants from the John Simon Guggenheim Foundation, the National Endowment for the Arts, and the Ingram Merrill Foundation. She was awarded the Witter Bynner Prize from the American Academy and Institute of Arts and Letters. She teaches at the University of Utah, where she directs the creative writing program. *"Tilia cordata"* will appear in *My Lookalike at the Krishna Temple*, forthcoming from LSU Press in 2019.

Of *"Tilia cordata,"* Osherow writes: "This poem—generated by the strange conjunction of a tremendous sense of disorientation and unease on my first visit to Germany and the jarring familiarity of Germany's iconic, ubiquitous tree—seems to me now to function as a sort of off-balance thumbnail autobiography. My parents each make an appearance, my daughters, my ex-husband, as well as the teacher who opened my nine-year-old eyes—in Hebrew—to the limitless possibilities of language. The poem tracks my lifelong habit of alternating between obsessive wandering and stationary dreaming as well as my exchange of a city full of green, green parks—where, from spring through summer, some floral scent (lilac, honeysuckle, rose) was always hanging on the humid air—for a parched, usually tawny, semidesert city in which one has to make a great effort to smell a flower. And casting its immeasurable pall over everything: the enduring ethnic shell shock into which I was born. I speak, of course, of the unassimilable horror of mid-twentieth-century Jewish history and the sense that I—undeservedly, through sheer luck and eleven years—had escaped, by the skin of my teeth, mass murder.

"I chose rhyming couplets—in which I'd written only one previous, much shorter poem—because I hoped they'd lend all this intensity a bit of restraint. I'm accustomed to writing long poems in terza rima and, to some degree, I see these rhyming couplets as a sort of austere, disciplined, perhaps foreshortened terza rima, replacing the forward-reaching intervening rhyme with silence.

"The personal inadequacies described in this poem—my complete inability to deal with Germany, German, or German people, my sense that I simply couldn't get out of Germany fast enough—ultimately didn't sit well with me. This poem became the genesis of the poems I've been writing for the past year. With the help of the University of Utah's Research Committee, the same committee that sent me to Darmstadt, I spent three months in Berlin in the hope of 'producing a series of poems in which I come to terms with and perhaps even modify and improve my tortured relationship with Germany.' What can I say? I'm working on it."

MIKE OWENS has been in prison for more than twenty years. A survivor of childhood abuse, he is serving a life-without-parole sentence in the maximum security prison in California, where he first read and wrote poetry. His journey of introspection and growth began there. He holds a certification for group counseling and is pursuing a degree in social and behavioral science. In 2010 he won the Pen American Dawson Prize for his poem "Black Settlement Photo: Circa 1867." He self-published his first book of poetry and essays, *Foreign Currency* (lulu.com, 2012). His latest book, *The Way Back* (2017), includes the poem "Sad Math" and is available from Random Lane Press (Sacramento, California; Randomlanepress@gmail.com).

Of "Sad Math," Owens writes: "This piece came from a very dense writing period. I was serving time at High Desert State Prison, which was, in the early 2000s, California's most violent maximum-security prison. Twenty-four hour confinement in a two-man cell regularly lasted months, and sometimes years on end. Acts of aggression and inhumanity were the norm, between staff and inmates alike. Poetry was for me a place where I could safeguard my humanity. I learned to look for, and capture, opportunities to reinforce my decision to not surrender to the cold. I may have been powerless to change the culture of violence around me, but by collecting moments of innocence and vulnerability, I was able to keep the best of me alive.

"Contrary to what people may take from the poem, Larry wasn't a naturally sympathetic figure. He was a fiftysomething, low-level member of a Los Angeles street gang. He was prone to fantastical lies for no apparent reason. He was perpetually in trouble with guards, or in debt to some other prisoner, and seemed uninterested in anything that wasn't instantly gratifying. Despite all of that, I could see the child in him that desperately wanted to be loved and valued. That is the part of him I held space for in the poem."

ELISE PASCHEN, who was born in Chicago, graduated from Harvard University and received her MPhil and DPhil degrees from Oxford University. She is the author of *The Nightlife* (Red Hen Press, 2017), *Bestiary* (Red Hen Press, 2009), *Infidelities* (Story Line Press, 1996), winner of the Nicholas Roerich Poetry Prize, and *Houses: Coasts* (Oxford: Sycamore Press, 1985). Paschen is coeditor of *Poetry in Motion* (W. W. Norton, 1996) and *Poetry Speaks* (Sourcebooks, 2001), and editor of *Poetry Speaks to Children* (Sourcebooks, 2005) and *Poetry Speaks Who I Am* (Sourcebooks, 2010). She is a former executive director of the Poetry Society of America and a cofounder of Poetry in Motion, a nation-wide program that places poetry posters in subways and buses. She teaches in the MFA Writing Program at the School of the Art Institute of Chicago.

Of "The Week Before She Died," Paschen writes: "This poem was drawn from a dream I had a week before my mother died, so I suppose it could be called a dream elegy, an occasion that allowed me to experience my mother young again. My mother was eighty-eight years old when she passed away and had been suffering from dementia for many years. During those months before her death I had been contemplating writing a prose piece about the summer when she and my father were separated—a period when my mother, the prima ballerina Maria Tall-chief, met and became romantically involved with the dancer Rudolph Nureyev and then introduced Nureyev to the dancer Erik Bruhn, with whom he fell in love. The dream, which served as a springboard for the poem, distilled the drama of these relationships into one scene. I have struggled to recall the elegance and brilliance of my mother before the onset of her dementia and writing this poem offered me a glimpse of her infatuation and of her resilience. 'The Week Before She Died' is included in my most recent book, *The Nightlife*, which is comprised of many dream narratives."

JESSICA PIAZZA teaches at the University of Southern California, where she received a PhD in English literature and creative writing. She is the author of two full-length poetry collections from Red Hen Press (*Interrobang* in 2013 and—with coauthor Heather Aimee O'Neill—*Obliterations* in 2016), as well as the 2014 chapbook *This is not a sky* from Black Lawrence Press. A cofounder of *Bat City Review* and Gold Line Press, she curates the website Poetry Has Value, which explores the intersections of poetry, money, and worth. She was awarded the Amy Clampitt Residency, which will begin in 2019. She is from Brooklyn, New York.

Piazza writes: "While 'Bells' Knells' generally fits my usual poetic style in terms of wordplay, rhythm, and rhyme, the subject matter is different from the majority of my work. I'm not a religious person . . . though the iconography, imagery, philosophy, and cultural impact of religion do show up in my work once in a while. However, I am attracted to people's obsession with and attachment to religion, and the ways religion can be used to justify behavior, both helpful and harmful. There's such darkness surrounding cultural notions of the Catholic Church right now, and I couldn't stop thinking about how the evil hidden within this ostensibly loving institution isn't so different from the darkness hidden in individuals, especially regarding personal relationships. Just as religions promise salvation, marriage (and other lifelong romantic commitments) have been offered up as another kind of saving; a way to escape our fears, our loneliness, the world's ridicule, and more. Marriage and religion both offer a sort of community, and in 'Bells' Knells,' the speaker realizes that her community is false at best and monstrous at worst. She must now ask herself what complicity she had in the darkness, and what signs she missed or pretended to miss. Whether the community in question is a personal one or a spiritual one is up to the reader. Thus, it's a strange little piece; both literal and metaphorical at once, a mingling of the theological and the personal. On one hand, I'm writing about a speaker considering her religion and its crimes. But I'm also writing about another speaker entirely; one considering her disastrous and broken marriage.

For me, they have equal weight in the poem, but are not fully themat-ically integrated. This double vision pleased me a lot, as do my con-tinued attempts to juxtapose the two themes to figure out how they illuminate each other. I don't have concrete answers, unfortunately. But, hey, do any of us?"

Born in 1973 in Grand Forks, North Dakota, AARON POOCHIGIAN earned a PhD in classics from the University of Minnesota and an MFA in poetry from Columbia University. His first book of poetry, *The Cosmic Purr* (Able Muse Press), was published in 2012. Winner of the 2016 Able Muse Poetry Prize, *Manhattanite*, his second book, came out in 2017 as did his thriller in verse, *Mr. Either/Or* (Etrus-can Press). *Stung with Love*, his book of translations from Sappho, was published in 2009, and his translation of Apollonius's *Jason and the Argonauts* in 2014, both from Penguin Classics. For his work in trans-lation he was awarded a 2010–2011 grant by the National Endow-ment for the Arts.

Poochigian writes: "One of the original femmes fatales, Salome danced for her father, King Herod II, on his birthday. Herod was so 'pleased' that he 'promised with an oath to give her whatsoever she would ask of him (Gospel of Matthew 14:6–11). At her mother Hero-dias's urging, Salome asked that he give her the head of John the Bap-tist on a dish. True to his word, Herod had John executed and his head brought on to Salome. In a form intended to be as sinuous as Salome's dance, my poem 'Happy Birthday, Herod' expresses, in the eternal present, well, quite a bit, I hope—the allure of living flesh, revulsion at dead flesh, the temptation to choose immediate titillation over moral-ity, and the ease with which one can remain a mere bystander in the face of an atrocity.

"I am far from the first poet to write on this theme. There is, of course, Mr. Prufrock's vision of his 'head (grown slightly bald) brought in upon a platter.' In one of the most gorgeously devastating poems ever written, 'Nineteen Hundred and Nineteen,' Yeats multi-plies Salome into the mysterious 'daughters of Herodias':

> Herodias' daughters have returned again,
> A sudden blast of dusty wind and after
> Thunder of feet, tumult of images
> Their purpose in the labyrinth of the wind."

Ruben Quesada was born in Los Angeles, California, in 1976. Dr. Quesada has taught writing, literature, and literary translation at Vermont College of Fine Arts and at Columbia College in Chicago. He is the author of *Next Extinct Mammal* (Greenhouse Review Press, 2011) and *Exiled from the Throne of Night: Selected Translations of Luis Cernuda* (Aureole Press, 2008).

Quesada writes: "The year I wrote 'Angels in the Sun' I was traveling to art museums. I had received a grant to write a book-length collection of ekphrastic poems. I visited museums from New York to San Francisco, Los Angeles to DC, Miami to Indianapolis, and so many more. I was drawn to naturalistic landscape paintings of the Romantic period and to American paintings of the late nineteenth century whose focus was urban landscapes.

"In early 2015, I visited the J. Paul Getty Museum in Los Angeles where I found an atmospheric scene painted by Joseph Mallord William Turner. The painting was *The Angel Standing in the Sun*. The tragic scene depicts Archangel Michael on Judgment Day foregrounded by other biblical figures. The canvas is covered in bright orange and yellow color—a fiery scene. Here in Turner's painting is a confluence of heaven and hell—the Apocalypse. My poem is an attempt to reinterpret that moment from a singular perspective located somewhere in the background.

"Turner's painting *The Angel Standing in the Sun* is part of the permanent exhibit at the Tate Britain in London but that spring it made its West Coast debut. The artwork was originally exhibited in London in 1846."

Alexandra Lytton Regalado was born in El Salvador in 1972. *Matria*, her book of poems, was the winner of the St. Lawrence Book Award (Black Lawrence Press, 2017). Cofounder of Kalina publishing, she has written, edited, or translated more than ten Central American–themed books including *Vanishing Points: Contemporary Salvadoran Prose* (2017). She received the 2015 Coniston Poetry Prize. Her photo-essay project about El Salvador, *through_the_bulletproof_glass*, is on Instagram. For more info visit: www.alexandralyttonregalado.com.

Of "La Mano," Regalado writes: "The poem takes place in El Salvador when I was in the beast mode of the new mom: breastfeeding round the clock, rawboned tired, overprotective and overwhelmed. Sure, caring for my son included moments that kicked the door open to wonder, spikes of joy, and at times an awe that felt like terror. But there was a sad undertone that I couldn't quite pin down until I put my firstborn's life in context with the exodus of more than 60,000 unaccompanied minors. In El Salvador parakeets were once very common; you'd see the green smear flash across the sky twice a day—as they left and returned to their roosts in the early mornings and at dusk. Nowadays those sightings are less constant as more trees are cut down to make room for the growing city. At the same time, more children are leaving their homeland—their parents hopeful, desperate for them to find someplace better, fully cognizant of the terrifying risk of that trip across the border. Richard Wilbur and Maya Angelou's words are flags of other exoduses, of other populations. For my son, it was the birds' flight that intrigued and fascinated him—not their staying there on the sill. He knew their beauty was in their ability to fly. I'm left watching the birds' departure with my child in my arms, thinking of those fleeing children, in wonder and terror, of how they will get there, if they get there, and how they will be received once they arrive."

Born in Seattle in 1970, PAISLEY REKDAL is the author of a book of essays, *The Night My Mother Met Bruce Lee* (Pantheon Books, 2000, and Vintage Books, 2002); a hybrid-genre photo-text entitled *Intimate: An American Family Photo Album* (Tupelo Books, 2012); and five books of poetry: *A Crash of Rhinos* (University of Georgia Press, 2000), *Six Girls Without Pants* (Eastern Washington University Press, 2002), *The Invention of the Kaleidoscope* (University of Pittsburgh Press, 2007), and *Animal Eye* (Pittsburgh, 2012), which won the UNT Rilke Prize. Her newest poetry collection is *Imaginary Vessels* (Copper Canyon Press, 2016), and her latest nonfiction work is *The Broken Country* (Georgia, 2017), which won the 2016 AWP Nonfiction Prize. Her work has received the Amy Lowell Poetry Traveling Scholarship, a Guggenheim Fellowship, and a Fulbright Fellowship. She teaches at the University of Utah and is Utah's poet laureate.

Rekdal writes: "I'm just finishing a book of poems, *Nightingale*, that rewrites several of the myths that appear in Ovid's *The Metamorphoses*. 'Philomela' is one of the first I wrote, and is also—for the reader of Ovid—a fairly big departure. In Ovid's version, Philomela is not only raped but dismembered, as Tereus (Philomela's rapist and brother-in-law) cuts out her tongue. Philomela is able to tell her sister about her violation because she weaves a tapestry that depicts the crime; later, this tapestry sets in motion another series of horrific events that culminates in the transformation of Philomela into a nightingale: Western symbol for lyric poetry. For me, the myth is about art, violence, and voicelessness, in particular the conflicted roles that art—and particularly poetry—play in the communication of trauma.

" 'Philomela' also has a companion piece I wrote, entitled 'Nightingale: A Gloss.' My gloss deconstructs Ovid's myth, my own retelling of it, and traces the literary evolution of the nightingale symbol. It's a very personal essay, too, since it addresses a violent assault I experienced years ago. For me, 'Philomela' is part of a long conversation I've been having—with literature, and with myself—about violence. It's a myth that's meant a lot to me over the years, one I've argued with, and feared, and rejected, and admired. I think I will struggle with it for the rest of my life."

MICHAEL ROBBINS was born in Topeka, Kansas, during the Vietnam War. Raised in Kansas and Colorado, he holds a PhD in English from the University of Chicago and is assistant professor of English and creative writing at Montclair State University. His poetry books are *Alien vs. Predator* (Penguin, 2012) and *The Second Sex* (Penguin, 2014). A book of essays, *Equipment for Living: On Poetry and Pop Music*, was published by Simon & Schuster in 2017.

Robbins writes: " 'Walkman' came about because I was bored with the sort of poem I'd been writing. I resolved to do everything differently, formally and thematically—to mostly eschew rhyme, for instance, and to risk vulnerability. This entailed some flailing about for a few months, until I hit on the idea of immersing myself in the work of a poet as different from me as I could imagine. I ended up reading James Schuyler's *Selected Poems* front to back. I'd always preferred Ashbery and O'Hara, but this time Schuyler broke something open in me. 'Walkman' doesn't sound much like Schuyler—his confident medley of digression and surprise is inimitable—but he was its impetus. Along with the desire not to stay in one place. I wrote it in one long burst over about nine hours, which never happened before and hasn't happened since."

J. ALLYN ROSSER was born in Bethlehem, Pennsylvania, in 1957. She has published four collections of poems, most recently *Mimi's Trapeze*

(University of Pittsburgh Press, 2014). She has received fellowships from the Guggenheim Foundation, the National Endowment for the Arts, and the Lannan Foundation. She teaches at Ohio University, where for eight years she served as editor of the *New Ohio Review*.

Of "Personae Who Got Loose," Rosser writes: "Henry James often drew on bits of gossip heard at dinner parties to generate his characters and launch his plots. But he complained that all too often he was not able to stop the teller in time—too many facts were offered, which ruined the 'virus of suggestion,' 'the wandering word, the vague echo,' and spoiled the artistic process. 'One's subject,' he said, 'is the merest grain, the speck of truth, of beauty, of reality, scarce visible to the common eye.' You can readily see James's desire to preserve mystery reflected in the character of Lambert Strether in *The Ambassadors*; Strether spends much of the novel trying not to learn too much about the very thing he has been sent abroad to investigate. 'Personae Who Got Loose' provides only the stray suggestive grains of its personae, in an effort to prevent the essentially reductive effect of fleshing out—to save them even from their own desire to be narrated to death."

MARY RUEFLE was born in McKeesport, Pennsylvania, in 1952. Her latest book is *My Private Property* (Wave Books, 2016). Vermont has been her home since 1971.

Of "Genesis," Ruefle writes: "When I look at this poem now, I think I may have been reading the Bible (I like very much reading the Bible but seldom 'have the time'), because the words 'and' and 'then' appear most frequently in that book; I don't rightly remember, but the title, surely, is another clue. It is only now that I see the poem may be read in a political context, as if its subtext were our great environmental crisis. Another take on it could be that the poem alludes to the election of our own President Trump, but neither of these things were on my mind when I wrote the poem. That often happens, you know— one looks back and sees multiple readings of a poem they thought was 'about' something else; in any case, events unfold in the poem, some very big things happen, and presumably some things are going to happen in the future when the girl children and boy children come together and make more children."

KAY RYAN was born in California in 1945. She has published nine books of poetry, including *Elephant Rocks* (1996), *Say Uncle* (2000),

The Niagara River (2005), *The Best of It: New and Selected Poems* (2010), and *Erratic Facts* (2015) all from Grove Press. *The Best of It* was awarded the Pulitzer Prize in 2011. She served as Poet Laureate of the United States from 2008 to 2010.

Of "Some Transcendent Addiction to the Useless," Ryan writes: "I cannot hope to attain the transcendent uselessness George Steiner attributes only to 'a handful of human beings' (Mozart for one), but perhaps I will have occasionally managed the undoing of a few things that needed it. This poem hopes that."

MARY JO SALTER was born in Grand Rapids, Michigan, in 1954. She is the author of eight books of poems published by Knopf, most recently *Nothing by Design* (2013) and *The Surveyors* (2017). She is the editor of *The Selected Poems of Amy Clampitt* (Knopf, 2010) and has been coeditor for three editions of *The Norton Anthology of Poetry*, including the sixth edition, published by W. W. Norton in 2018. Her poems have been set to music by Caroline Shaw (in a world premiere sung by Renee Fleming) and by Fred Hersch (in the song cycle *Rooms of Light: The Life of Photographs*). Salter is Krieger-Eisenhower Professor in The Writing Seminars at Johns Hopkins University, and lives in Baltimore.

Salter writes: "I can't count how often a spoonerism, a malapropism, or a misheard expression has jump-started a line of poetry for me—or even a whole poem. This was the case for 'We'll Always Have Parents.' I must have thought of Humphrey Bogart's reassurance to Ingrid Bergman in *Casablanca* ('We'll always have Paris') a thousand times before I heard that last word as 'parents,' and laughed out loud. Did the phrase suddenly twist because, in the past few years, I've had the unfunny experience of watching a nonagenarian father decline into dementia? Was the poem a gesture toward accepting that I would *not* always have a father? In any case, the poem (which came in a rush) is also a celebration of the great Hollywood melodramas—a source of ever-fresh entertainment for both my father and me."

JASON SCHNEIDERMAN was born in San Antonio, Texas, in 1976, and is the author of *Primary Source* (Red Hen Press, 2016), *Striking Surface* (Ashland Poetry Press, 2010), and *Sublimation Point* (Four Way Books, 2004), as well as the editor of *Queer: A Reader for Writers* (Oxford University Press, 2016). He is an associate professor of English at the

Borough of Manhattan Community College, CUNY. His husband, Michael Broder, is the publisher of Indolent Books.

Schneiderman writes: "I had known that 3-D printing was based on some kind of tiny blocklike unit, but when I first saw the word 'voxel' (a portmanteau of 'volume' and 'pixel'), the connection between 2-D screens and these newly printable objects sort of blew my mind.

"Over the course of my life, I've watched pixels get smaller and smaller. My first pixels were on the video game *Centipede* at a laundromat in England on a console designed for two players sitting opposite each other, with a screen facing up through a glass tabletop. The images of the quick moving arachnids, insects, and lasers were composed of giant moving dots. To be honest, video games held very little fascination for me. I only truly began to pay attention when we had a home computer, and the pixels had shrunk enough to form glowing green letters against a black screen, composing texts that could be printed up on a dot matrix printer. From there, it was a steady progression to ink jet and laser jet printers, to WYSIWYG ('what you see is what you get') word processing programs, to laptop computers, to notebook computers, to smartphones, to tablets. It would seem that the pixel reached its final size in Apple's 2012 Retina Display, which promised a pixel so small as to be indistinguishable to the human eye. The word 'voxel' put me at the start of a vertiginous new evolution, though one that felt predictable. I'd seen this movie before: as the unit gets smaller and more accessible, it becomes increasingly integrated into the fabric of your life.

"The day I learned that this poem would find new life in *The Best American Poetry*, I happened to walk past a store offering 3-D printed figurines of yourself and your loved ones. You stand in a cross between an airport scanner and an elephant cage to be scanned from all sides, and you get a slightly fuzzy, delicately colored version of yourself. So that part of the poem is already coming true. Still, as of this writing, 'voxel' is not in the *Oxford English Dictionary*."

Born in St. Thomas, in the US Virgin Islands, and raised in Apopka, Florida, NICOLE SEALEY is the author of *Ordinary Beast* (Ecco, 2017) and *The Animal After Whom Other Animals Are Named* (Northwestern University Press, 2016), winner of the 2015 Drinking Gourd Chapbook Poetry Prize. She has also won an Elizabeth George Foundation Grant, the Stanley Kunitz Memorial Prize from *The American Poetry Review*, a Daniel Varoujan Award and the Poetry International Prize, as well as fellowships from CantoMundo, Cave Canem Foundation, MacDowell Colony and the Poetry Project. She holds an MLA in Africana Studies from the University of South Florida and an MFA in creative writing from New York University. She is the executive director at the Cave Canem Foundation.

MICHAEL SHEWMAKER was born in Texarkana, Texas, in 1979. His first collection of poems, *Penumbra*, won the 2016 Hollis Summers Poetry Prize and was published by Ohio University Press in 2017. He is a Jones Lecturer in poetry at Stanford University.

Shewmaker writes: "'Advent' started with a scene I witnessed at an advent service at Stanford Memorial Church. The balconies were opened because of the crowd and during one of the hymns a boy tried to pull himself onto the railing. His mother was attentive, though, and caught him before any harm was done. That moment stayed with me and I couldn't help but wonder what would have happened if she had looked away, if only for a moment. At that point, the metaphor—between the boy and Christ—was unavoidable and the poem largely unfolded on its own."

CARMEN GIMÉNEZ SMITH is the author of a memoir and six poetry collections, including *Milk and Filth* (University of Arizona Press, 2013). Her most recent poetry collection is *Cruel Futures* (City Lights Publishers, 2018) and *Be Recorder* is forthcoming from Graywolf Press in 2019. She is coeditor of *Angels of the Americlypse: New Latin@ Writing*, an anthology of contemporary Latinx writing (Counterpath Press, 2014). She is chair of the planning committee for CantoMundo and is the publisher of Noemi Press. She is professor of English at Virginia Tech and, with Stephanie Burt, poetry editor of *The Nation*.

Of "Dispatch from Midlife," Smith writes: "I wrote this poem to describe what being 'midlife' actually means to me, a quick take, but also a message to a younger me. When I was a teen in California and went dancing at One Step Beyond (RIP), I'd always see a guy who looked like a forty-year-old Klaus Kinski in MC Hammer pants dancing like his life depended on it. I watched him with wonder and disbelief from a very selective puritanical stance about what spaces were appropriate for young people versus older people. I saw midlife as a boring space of work, family, and waiting for death. Now, when I see a face of someone my age (forty-seven) or even older, I see the younger face in that face—like I have a new superpower. I can see all the people they've been, and I see it with love and loyalty having also grown and changed and widened. I also see the younger person in my current face, and only occasionally feel the self-loathing women my age are conditioned to feel, but, most importantly, I feel like I *am* still myself at twenty, at thirty, at forty. She is still in me and has mostly not changed despite what my body looks like after giving birth, feeding my children with my body, illness, and aging. I know more about the world, and I know that if I wanted to go to dance like no one was looking, someone might be looking, but IDGAF. I'm this thing that I made with time and work and error and triumph. I'm also relieved by the freedom of being able to wear a caftan or long flowy scarves, and that's where the wanton indifference comes in. I would add, however, that for a minute the last line read 'sexual indifference,' but that's not exactly true. I'm still pretty sexy and sexual predation is about power, not beauty or age."

TRACY K. SMITH is the author of the memoir *Ordinary Light* (Knopf, 2015) and four books of poetry, including *Life on Mars* (Graywolf Press, 2011), winner of the Pulitzer Prize, and *Wade in the Water* (Graywolf, 2018). She is the twenty-second Poet Laureate of the United States, and a professor at Princeton University.

Of "An Old Story," Smith writes: "I wrote this poem thinking it might be nice to take a stab at creating a new myth. Instead of brushing aside my own sometimes-bleak feelings about the failings of the twenty-first century, I tried to embrace them, and fashion them into a story that culminates in humankind finding its way to a compassionate existence."

GARY SNYDER was born in San Francisco in 1930 and attended elementary schools in Seattle and Portland. He received his BA from Reed College in 1951 and studied East Asian languages at UC Berkeley between 1953 and 1956; during this period he also worked in the logging industry, and for the US Forest Service as a fire lookout. For many years he studied Buddhism in Japan. From 1986 to 2002 he taught at UC Davis, where he is now professor emeritus of English. He has received the Bollingen Prize, the Shelley Memorial Award from the Poetry Society of America, a Guggenheim Fellowship, and the Pulitzer Prize for *Turtle Island* (New Directions, 1974). His most recent collection of poems is *This Present Moment* (Counterpoint, 2015).

Of "Why California Will Never Be Like Tuscany," Snyder writes: "One early autumn in 2011 or so, I was visiting with Giuseppe Moretti, who's active with the Italian Bioregional Movement and who lives and works a historic farm quite near the Po River. I also spent some days at Etain Addey's sprawling farm project nearby. I couldn't help but see the parallels between this part of Italy (which surely had been a mixed forest of drought-adapted bushes and trees in preagricultural times) and earlier California. The numerous large fireproof stone and plaster farmhouses—many vacant—are instructive. And I thought about how the American West Coast over the next millennium will probably go through a similar process, but the houses won't last that long. I'm not sure which I'd favor."

A. E. STALLINGS, born in 1968, studied classics in Athens, Georgia, and has lived in Athens, Greece, since 1999. Awarded a MacArthur Fellowship, she has recently published a new verse translation of Hesiod's *Works and Days* with Penguin Classics. *Like*, a new volume of poems, is forthcoming from Farrar, Straus and Giroux.

Of "Pencil," Stallings writes: "Writing about this poem on a computer (not with a pencil, although the poem was drafted in pencil), I'm given to wonder whether the central metaphor will be easily understood in a decade or so. I have poems about landline telephones that perhaps now need explanations to be grasped by the very young! But I think the pencil, like print itself, is here to stay, it is so simple and elegant a technology. I am somewhat haunted by school and office supplies, perhaps because these are deep, powerful memories, stirred up by a stint of school teaching and then again by my own children's school-going. Getting out of one's seat to sharpen a pencil was sometimes the only moment of pure escape into daydreaming in those faraway classrooms, and maybe the nursery-rhyme ballad swing to this (as well as that it is almost a riddle with the answer in the title) comes from childhood.

"Among other office/school supply poems that come to mind are Elizabeth Bishop's '12 O'clock News' and Cavafy's early poem on an inkwell. But probably back, back in my mind the poem that makes this one possible is one by Roethke. I worked briefly in London in 1990 as a 'tea girl' at the Institute of Classical Studies, then in Gordon Square, and when I didn't walk, took the Tube from Warren Street Station. My roommate and I lived around the corner from Fitzroy Square, once home to Virginia Woolf. I dreamed of being a writer. Among the advertisements on the Tube was the series of Poems on the Underground. At least two of those poems ended up laying down formative strata in my young poet brain: Robert Graves's 'Love without Hope' and Theodore Roethke's 'Dolor,' which begins 'I have known the inexorable sadness of pencils.' I have often regretted that I didn't just up and steal one of those posters. Maybe I am still trying."

Born in Cambridge, England, of American parents in 1933, ANNE STEVENSON was brought up and educated in Ann Arbor, Michigan. Graduating from the University of Michigan in 1954 with a major Hopwood Award, she later published two collections of poetry with Wesleyan University Press, including an epistolary novel in verse called *Correspondences* (1974)—the first of ten collections to appear from Oxford University Press between 1974 and 1996. In 1998, after OUP stopped publishing new poetry, she moved with her family to Durham in the northeast of England and brought out two more collections with Bloodaxe Books in Newcastle before publishing in 2006 a more or less up-to-date *Poems 1955–2005*. She observes: "It was probably this hefty volume and its reviews that prompted the Poetry Foundation of America to remember that I was still an American and to present me with the Neglected Masters Award in 2007." This honor was confirmed in 2008 by a *Selected Poems* in the American Poets Project series, sponsored by the Library of America, and a Life Achievement Award from the Lannan Foundation. Since then, Bloodaxe Books has published two more collections, *Stone Milk* (2007) and *Astonishment* (2012).

Of "How Poems Arrive," Stevenson writes: "At eighty-five, I am still writing poems, but fewer as I become older, slower, crazier, and more fastidious. My latest Bloodaxe publication is a book of lectures delivered in the past five or six years called *About Poems: and how poems are not about*. The title and to some extent all the lectures in this book dwell on and demonstrate how word-sounds and bodily rhythms (heartbeat and breathing) recorded in the accents of a language are essential to poetry. Although I didn't write 'How Poems Arrive' with the purpose of using it as a preface to my arguments, when it was written I realized that my conscious and unconscious mind had been working in tandem to find a resonant form of words that would explain something of the mystery of how poems (real poems, gut poems) force themselves into being. Of course, poems are written for many reasons and for a variety of purposes. But if you are really and helplessly a poet, I'm sure lines often arrive, as it were, readymade, without your knowing why or how. It is incumbent on you to take them on, write them down, and then worry yourself, maybe half consciously or half asleep, until you find a form that will help you bring them to the surface. In the case of 'How Poems Arrive' it was deciding to write the poem in terza rima that helped my conscious brain to listen to what the poem was saying."

ADRIENNE SU is the author of four books of poems, *Middle Kingdom* (Alice James Books, 1997), *Sanctuary* (Manic D Press, 2006), *Having None of It* (Manic D, 2009), and *Living Quarters* (Manic D, 2015). Born in Atlanta, Georgia, in 1967, she studied at Harvard and Radcliffe Colleges and the University of Virginia and has held fellowships from The Frost Place, the Fine Arts Work Center in Provincetown, and the National Endowment for the Arts. She is professor of creative writing and poet-in-residence at Dickinson College, in Carlisle, Pennsylvania. Links to poems and prose are available at adriennesu.ink.

Of "Substitutions," Su writes: "I have long surrounded myself with two genres of books, poetry, and cookbooks, interests I usually consider separate and at odds. Over time, however, the language of cooking instruction has expanded my approach to poetry. The imperative voice evokes intimacy, a guiding hand, and possibly the voice of a late grandmother, while legitimizing second-person narration. That the shorthand of recipe writing—'soft peaks,' 'a lively simmer,' 'pliable dough'—parallels the pointers writers give each other in revision—'trust the reader,' 'starts in the middle,' 'ending too pat'—helps validate home cooking as an art form and makes it, in some small way, less of a violation of writing time. Meanwhile, I read cookbooks in part for pleasure, but also to inhabit the matrilineal history that otherwise seems to be missing. Unlike canonized literature, cookbooks are a genre in which the reader can go back in time and not find that the default pronoun has become an unquestioned 'he.' Although the cook in 'Substitutions' is male, he shares with most female cooks of the past the anonymity of the local or domestic artist.

"The description of the Sichuan noodle dish *dan dan mian* in Fuchsia Dunlop's meticulously researched *Land of Plenty* brought about this poem by making me hungry, less for noodles than for the adventure of imagining noodles. Trying to give coherent shape to what I pictured became a chance to link rhymed couplets to a form that might otherwise be seen as purely functional, the ingredient-substitution list. The process also revealed a need to explore one of the ghost dishes that seemed to dwell in and around my childhood, both of my parents having immigrated, long before I was born, from China to the American South, where Asian Americans were so few that the term 'Asian American' had not reached us. Most days, my family's kitchen table appeared quite assimilated. Yet behind our deviled eggs hovered the specter of tea eggs; behind our morning oatmeal lay the comfort of congee; behind our weeknight spaghetti and meat sauce lurked a street vendor's noodles, cooked to order just about anywhere, day or night, in a place that lived mostly in memory."

NATASHA TRETHEWEY was born in Gulfport, Mississippi, in 1966. She served two terms as the nineteenth Poet Laureate of the United States (2012–2014) and is the author of four collections of poetry: *Domestic Work* (Graywolf Press, 2000), *Bellocq's Ophelia* (Graywolf, 2002), *Native Guard* (Houghton Mifflin, 2006)—for which she was awarded the 2007 Pulitzer Prize—and *Thrall* (Houghton Mifflin Harcourt, 2012). In 2010 she published a book of nonfiction, *Beyond Katrina: A Meditation on the Mississippi Gulf Coast* (University of Georgia Press). *Monument*, a volume of new and selected poems, is forthcoming from Houghton Mifflin Harcourt in 2018. She has received fellowships from the Academy of American Poets, the National Endowment for the Arts, the Guggenheim Foundation, the Rockefeller Foundation, the Beinecke Library at Yale, and the Radcliffe Institute for Advanced Study at Harvard. In 2013 she was inducted into the American Academy of Arts and Sciences, and in 2017 she received the Heinz Award for Arts and Humanities. At Northwestern University she is Board of Trustees Professor of English.

Of "Shooting Wild," Trethewey writes: "I have been working on this poem for twenty years. I began writing it in 1997, twelve years after my mother's death, in an attempt to explore why the sound of her voice was the part of my memory of her that I began to lose first. Once, a few years after she was gone, I found an old cassette recording of her speaking. I put the tape in the cassette player and she came back to me, vividly, for a few moments. Then the tape snagged and no matter how many times I took it out, unraveled and rewound it, it would no longer play. It caught again and again on the reels until it snapped."

AGNIESZKA TWOREK was born in Lublin, Poland, in 1975. She came to the United States with her family when she was eighteen. She received a BA in romance languages and literature from the University of Chicago and a PhD in French from Yale. She lives in Vermont.

Of "Grief Runs Untamed," Tworek writes: "I witnessed tanks and military trucks driving down the street behind my apartment building after martial law was declared in Poland when I was a child. This image has haunted me for years, reminding me that freedom and peace are fragile, and that war may be lurking around every corner. I have realized that it is important to look out the window of one's own life, to see what is beyond it, to observe what is happening in the larger world, to be a witness. I was fortunate to be accepted as an immigrant in the United States in 1993, yet I am aware that many displaced people around the world today are not welcome anywhere. My poem 'Grief Runs Untamed' attempts to chronicle the plight of such people, who have been brutally uprooted from their lives in so many places because of wars, drought, tyranny, gang violence, and religious and ethnic persecution. I wrote it as an elegy for the countless lives lost, for people who may never reach safety, and for those forced into exile and makeshift existences, who may never feel at home anywhere.

"Initially, I included the phrase 'grief runs untamed' in one of the lines of the poem; grief in that earlier version was confined to the abandoned houses. However, in the present version, the grief is much larger: the refugees and the world are its captives. It is boundless, and so it became the title of my poem."

G. C. WALDREP (b. 1968 in South Boston, Virginia) is the author most recently of a lyric collection, *feast gently* (Tupelo, 2018); a long poem, *Testament* (BOA Editions, 2015); and a chapbook, *Susquehanna* (Omnidawn, 2013). With Ilya Kaminsky, he is coeditor of *Homage to Paul Celan* (Marick Press, 2011); he and Joshua Corey are editors of *The Arcadia Project: North American Postmodern Pastoral* (Ahsahta Press, 2012).

He lives in Lewisburg, Pennsylvania, where he teaches at Bucknell University, edits the journal *West Branch*, and serves as editor at large for *The Kenyon Review*.

Of "Dear Office in Which I Must Account for Tears," Waldrep writes: "I drafted this poem on 22 November 2013 in Marfa, Texas—I owe a great debt to the Lannan Foundation, which enabled me to live and write there for six taut weeks. At the time, I was battling neurological issues that were perhaps Parkinsonian, perhaps not—not, in the end, though I would not know that with any certainty until mid-2015. (Keith Waldrop: 'I had not realized how dark it is, inside the body.') I was also rereading Darwish and Reverdy, in translation, while struggling with the emotional and spiritual fallout of a failed courtship. All or none of these conditions may be relevant to the poem, which surprised me, as the gift-poems always do. It arrived verbatim in the form in which it was later published, less two excised stanzas. It was the first of seven poems that day—a red-letter day, a very good day, we all hope for such days."

WANG PING was born in China and came to the United States in 1986. Her publications of poetry and prose include *American Visa* (Coffee House Press, 2008), *Foreign Devil* (Coffee House, 1996), *Of Flesh & Spirit* (Coffee House, 1998), *Aching for Beauty: Footbinding in China* (Anchor, 2002), *The Last Communist Virgin* (Coffee House, 2007), and *Life of Miracles along the Yangtze and Mississippi* (2017 AWP Nonfiction Award, University of Georgia Press, 2018). She has received the Eugene Kayden Award, a grant from the National Endowment for the Arts, the Bush Artist Fellowship for poetry, and the McKnight Fellowship for nonfiction. She was awarded the Distinct Immigrant Award in 2014 and was named Venezuela International Poet of Honor in 2015. A photographer and installation artist, she has had multimedia installations (*Behind the Gate: After the Flood of the Three Gorges* and *We Are Water: Kinship of Rivers* at Macalester College, Soap Factory Gallery, All My Relatives Gallery, Great River Museums, Bologna Art Gallery, Emily Carr Institute of Arts, and festivals in China, India, Peru, Venezuela, Nepal, and Canada). She is a professor of English at Macalester College and is the founder and director of the Kinship of Rivers project.

Of "*Lao Jia*," Wang Ping writes: "I was born and grew up in Shanghai, and have been living in USA since 1986. My official Chinese residence is still registered as Shandong, Weihai, my *lao jia*, my old home, my identity.

"Every Chinese belongs to *lao jia*, the land of our ancestors, our name, spirit, roots, no matter where we go, how far we wander.

"I left home at fourteen, to work as a farmer in a fishing village on the island of East China Sea, in pursuit of my college dream. I never went back home.

"Three years later, I left the village to study English at Hangzhou Language School. I never went back to the island.

"I left Hangzhou for Beijing University. My college dream came true at twenty-two.

"I left China in 1986, and never went back.

"My ex-boyfriend screamed repeatedly: 'Go back where you came from!!!' Still, I never went back.

"I got farther and farther away, carrying Weihai, my *lao jia*, my old home, in my dreams and thoughts.

"When I was fifty, I took my sons to visit my old home on the shore of the Yellow Sea, for the first time.

"Factories and luxury buildings take over the place my father talked about every day. The wheat fields are gone. The village is gone. The sand beach is gone. My grandma's grave, somehow, remains in the yam fields. I sit down in front of her stone, and everything floods back and up: memories, sorrow, joy, her voice and stories, my father's longing. . . .

"I look at my sons. They are eating steamed bread, for the first time in their life, but they devour it as if it were their daily meal since birth, as if they were slurping Cheerios and milk. This is the bread my father craved all his life while living on the island of the East China Sea as a navy officer.

"My sons are tied to the ancestral land, even though they were born in NYC and Midwest prairie, even though they love pizza, play hockey and baseball, and speak little Chinese.

"We all belong to *lao jia*, old home, old land, that is part of us.

"We carry home 家 in our chests, as we wander, from continent to continent, from sea to sea."

JAMES MATTHEW WILSON was born in East Lansing, Michigan, in 1975, and now lives in Pennsylvania, where he is associate professor of religion and literature in the department of humanities and Augustinian traditions at Villanova University. He is the author of seven books, including, most recently, *The Vision of the Soul: Truth, Goodness, and Beauty in the Western Tradition* (Catholic University of America Press, 2017), and a collection of poems, *Some Permanent Things* (Wiseblood Books, 2014). A two-time winner of the Lionel Basney Award from the Conference on Christianity and Literature, he was awarded the 2017 Hiett Prize by the Dallas Institute of Humanities and Culture, which recognizes younger scholars who are making significant contributions to the shaping of contemporary culture.

Of "On a Palm," Wilson writes: "Years ago, I used to walk my oldest daughter to school every morning, and we would pass by the local psychic and palm reader's shop. With its shabby exterior and big black sign out front, it seemed such an entrancing symbol of an age that has lost the bearings of genuine religious belief and has fallen, in consequence, into the decay of hokey superstitions. It is of course consoling to know that human nature does not change and that the mind cannot help but seek out a knowledge that transcends our everyday uses, even if it must do so in embarrassing ways. But there is also something a bit contemptible in the frequent settling for claptrap—claptrap pressed, moreover, into doing poor service for our psychological needs, when we should rather be offering ourselves in service to the truth itself. One day, not so long ago, I was driving past that shop and saw it had gone out of business. I set out to write a poem that portrayed just such a snarl of contempt, and I was delighted to see that it could find expression alongside candid acknowledgment of and sympathy for how badly our souls want to be known, cherished, taken into hand and held."

RYAN WILSON was born in Griffin, Georgia, in 1982, and raised in nearby Macon. He holds degrees from the University of Georgia, Johns Hopkins University, and Boston University. *The Stranger World*, his first book (Measure Press, 2017), won the Donald Justice Poetry Prize. He is the editor of *Literary Matters* (www.literarymatters.org) and the office manager of the Association of Literary Scholars, Critics, and Writers (ALSCW). He teaches at the Catholic University of America, where he is completing his doctorate. He and his wife, Kelly, live in Parkville, Maryland.

Wilson writes: " 'Face It' was written in West Virginia at a mountaintop cabin belonging to my great friend, Ernest Suarez. During a break near dusk, I stepped out onto the porch, from which one can see more than fifty miles on a clear day. I was tantalized by a hawk hovering in a western gap, how it seemed to approach and to recede at once on the wind, never near enough for me to identify its species, or even its genus.

"The season, the bird, and perhaps my own uncertainties about the future recalled to mind Robert Penn Warren's poem, 'Heart of Autumn,' a meditation on transformation that brilliantly transforms Horace's Ode ii.20, itself a poem of transformation.

"The form of 'Face It' is the bref double, a French predecessor of the sonnet that has rarely been brought into English. Writing 'Face It,' I knew of no English-language examples. I chose the form because it seems to be both a sonnet and not a sonnet, inhabiting a kind of formal liminal state that I hoped would parallel my poem's concerns with identity and transformation, being and becoming, selfhood and otherness.

"The choice of form derived from my study of Horace. In Ode ii.20, Horace refers to himself as a *biformis vates*, a 'two-form poet,' and he does so in part because he is bringing the Alcaic meter, a Greek form, into Latin-language poetry, and in part because the poem recounts the poet's own transformation into a swan. The transformation in content matches the transformation of the form. While lacking Horace's self-assurance, I hoped to create an analogous 'two-form' effect with my bref double, which, like the other poems in *The Stranger World*, seeks to promote what the ancient Greeks called ξενία (*xenia*), 'hospitality to the stranger,' whether that stranger be another individual or one's self."

CHRISTIAN WIMAN was born in West Texas in 1966. He is the author, editor, and translator of numerous books, including *Hammer Is the Prayer: Selected Poems* (Farrar, Straus and Giroux, 2016) and *Joy: 100 Poems* (Yale University Press, 2017). He teaches at the Yale Institute of Sacred Music and Yale Divinity School.

Of "Assembly," Wiman writes: "What is the point of poetry when the world is going to hell? I asked that question in an essay several years ago, but it has become even more urgent to me recently, now that the demons have taken off their masks and every day's news is a storm of slime and vileness. It surprises me, then, to find that my hope for poetry has actually increased—or perhaps simply *hardened*—right along with my rage. This is a poem of despair, but I hope its despair is prophetic rather than futile, furious and galvanizing rather than recessive and resigned. Faith in language is faith enough in times like these."

MAGAZINES WHERE THE POEMS
WERE FIRST PUBLISHED

Academic Questions, poetry ed. Felicia Sanzari Chernesky. www.nas.org/
projects/projects_academic_questions

The Adroit Journal, poetry eds. Jesse De Angelis, Lisa Hiton, Jackson
Holbert, and Talin Tahajian. www.theadroitjournal.org

Ambit, poetry eds. Ralf Webb, Imogen Cassels, and Ruby Silk. www
.ambitmagazine.co.uk

America, poetry ed. Joseph Hoover, SJ. www.americamagazine.org

The American Journal of Poetry, ed. Robert Nazarene, senior ed. James
Wilson. www.theamericanjournalofpoetry.com

The American Poetry Review, ed. Elizabeth Scanlon. www.aprweb.org

The Antioch Review, poetry ed. Judith Hall. http://review.antiochcollege
.org/antioch-review-home-page

The Atlantic, poetry ed. David Barber. www.theatlantic.com

Bennington Review, ed. Michael Dumanis. www.benningtonreview.org

Birmingham Poetry Review, ed. Adam Vines. www.uab.edu/cas/english
publications/bpr

BuzzFeed, executive ed., culture, Saeed Jones. www.buzzfeed.com/
reader

Catamaran, poetry eds. Catherine Segurson and Zack Rogow. www.
catamaranliteraryreader.com

Colorado Review, poetry eds. Donald Revell, Sasha Steensen, and Mat-
thew Cooperman. www.coloradoreview.colostate.edu/colorado
-review

The Common, poetry ed. John Hennessy. www.thecommononline.org

Copper Nickel, poetry eds. Brian Barker and Nicky Beer. www.copper
-nickel.org

The Dark Horse, eds. Gerry Cambridge with Jennifer Goodrich and
Marcia Menter. www.thedarkhorsemagazine.com

Denver Quarterly, poetry ed. Bin Ramke. www.du.edu/denverquarterly

Ecotone, poetry ed. Hunter Hobbs. www.ecotonemagazine.org

Fifth Wednesday Journal, eds. James Ballowe, Nina Corwin, and Susan
Azar Porterfield. www.fifthwednesdayjournal.com

First Things, poetry ed. Paul Lake. www.firstthings.com

Green Mountains Review, ed. Elizabeth Powell, poetry ed. Didi Jackson. www.greenmountainsreview.com

Gulf Coast, poetry eds. Daniel Chu, Aza Pace, and Chelsea B. DesAutels. www.gulfcoastmag.org

The Hopkins Review, poetry ed. Greg Williamson. www.hopkinsreview.jhu.edu

The Hudson Review, ed. Paula Deitz. www.hudsonreview.com

The Literary Review, poetry eds. Craig Morgan Teicher and Michael Morse. www.theliteraryreview.org

Met Magazine, ed. Ian Christon. www2.mmu.ac.uk/metmagazine

Modern Haiku, ed. Paul Miller. www.modernhaiku.org

Narrative, poetry ed. Michael Wiegers. www.narrativemagazine.com

The Nation, poetry eds. Stephanie Burt and Carmen Giménez Smith. www.thenation.com

The New Criterion, poetry ed. David Yezzi. www.newcriterion.com

New England Review, poetry ed. Rick Barot. www.nereview.com

The New York Times Magazine, selected by Matthew Zapruder. www.nytimes.com/section/magazine

The New Yorker, poetry ed. Kevin Young. www.newyorker.com

The Paris Review, poetry ed. Robyn Creswell. www.theparisreview.org

Parnassus: Poetry in Review, ed. Herbert Leibowitz. www.parnassusreview.com

Plume, editor-in-chief Daniel Lawless. www.plumepoetry.com

Poet Lore, eds. Jody Bolz and E. Ethelbert Miller. www.poetlore.com

Poetry, ed. Don Share. www.poetryfoundation.org

Presence, ed. Mary Ann Buddenberg Miller with Lois Roma-Deeley and Marjorie Maddox. www.catholicpoetryjournal.com

Raritan, editor-in-chief Jackson Lears. www.raritanquarterly.rutgers.edu

Rattle, eds. Alan Fox and Timothy Green. www.rattle.com

Resistance, Rebellion, Life: 50 Poems Now (Knopf, 2017), ed. Amit Majmudar

Seneca Review, eds. David Weiss, Geoffrey Babbitt, and Kathryn Cowles. www.hws.edu/senecareview

The Sewanee Review, poetry ed. Robert Walker. www.thesewaneereview.com

Smartish Pace, ed. Stephen Reichert. www.smartishpace.com

The Southern Review, poetry ed. Jessica Faust. www.thesouthernreview.org

Southern Poetry Review, ed. James Smith. www.southernpoetryreview
.com

Southwest Review, editor-in-chief Greg Brownderville. www.smu.edu
/SouthwestReview

Southword, ed. Patrick Cotter. www.munsterlit.ie/Southword

The Sun, poetry ed. Carol Ann Fitzgerald. www.thesunmagazine.org

Think Journal, ed. David J. Rothman. www.think-journal.submittable
.com

The Threepenny Review, ed. Wendy Lesser. www.threepennyreview
.com

Tin House, poetry ed. Camille T. Dungy. www.tinhouse.com

Virginia Quarterly Review, poetry ed. Gregory Pardlo. www.vqronline
.org

ACKNOWLEDGMENTS

The series editor thanks Mark Bibbins for his invaluable assistance. Warm thanks go also to Stacey Harwood, Thomas Moody, and Virginia Valenzuela; to Glen Hartley and Lynn Chu of Writers' Representatives; and to Ashley Gilliam, David Stanford Burr, Daniel Cuddy, Erich Hobbing, and Patrick Weir at Scribner.

Grateful acknowledgment is made of the publications in which these poems first appeared and the editors who selected them. A sincere attempt has been made to locate all copyright holders. Unless otherwise noted, copyright to the poems is held by the individual poets.

Allison Adair, "Miscarriage" from *Southwest Review*. Reprinted by permission of the poet.

Kaveh Akbar, "Against Dying" from *Calling a Wolf a Wolf* © 2017 by Kaveh Akbar. Reprinted by permission of The Permissions Company, Inc., on behalf of Alice James Books. Also appeared in *Tin House*.

Julia Alvarez, "American Dreams" from *America*. Reprinted by permission of the poet.

A. R. Ammons, "Finishing Up" from *The Complete Poems of A. R. Ammons: Volume 2, 1978–2005* © 2017 by the Estate of A. R. Ammons. Reprinted by permission of W. W. Norton & Co. Also appeared in *Poetry*.

David Barber, "Sherpa Song" from *Southwest Review*. Reprinted by permission of the poet.

Andrew Bertaina, "A Translator's Note" from *The Threepenny Review*. Reprinted by permission of the poet.

Frank Bidart, "Mourning What We Thought We Were" from *The New Yorker*. Reprinted by permission of the poet.

Bruce Bond, "Anthem" from *Denver Quarterly*. Reprinted by permission of the poet.

George Bradley, "Those Were the Days" from *Raritan*. Reprinted by permission of the poet.

Joyce Clement, "Birds Punctuate the Days" from *Modern Haiku*. Reprinted by permission of the poet.

Brendan Constantine, "The Opposites Game" from *The American Journal of Poetry*. Reprinted by permission of the poet.

Maryann Corbett, "Prayer Concerning the New, More 'Accurate' Translation of Certain Prayers" from *Rattle*. Reprinted by permission of the poet.

Robert Cording, "Toast to My Dead Parents" from *The Sewanee Review*. Reprinted by permission of the poet.

Cynthia Cruz, "Artaud" from *Bennington Review*. Reprinted by permission of the poet.

Dick Davis, "A Personal Sonnet" from *The Hudson Review*. Reprinted by permission of the poet.

Warren Decker, "Today's Special" from *Think Journal*. Reprinted by permission of the poet.

Susan de Sola, "The Wives of the Poets" from *The Dark Horse*. Reprinted by permission of the poet.

Dante Di Stefano, "Reading Dostoyevsky at Seventeen" from *Met Magazine*. Reprinted by permission of the poet.

Nausheen Eusuf, "Pied Beauty" from *Birmingham Poetry Review*. Reprinted by permission of the poet.

Jonathan Galassi, "Orient Epithalamion" from *The New Yorker*. Reprinted by permission of the poet.

Jessica Goodfellow, "Test" from *The Southern Review*. Reprinted by permission of the poet.

Sonia Greenfield, "Ghost Ship" from *Rattle*. Reprinted by permission of the poet.

Joy Harjo, "An American Sunrise" from *Poetry*. Reprinted by permission of the poet.

Terrance Hayes, "American Sonnet for My Past and Future Assassin" from *American Sonnets for My Past and Future Assassin* © 2018 by Terrance Hayes. Reprinted by permission of Penguin Random House. Also appeared in *The New Yorker*.

Ernest Hilbert, "Mars Ultor" from *Academic Questions*. Reprinted by permission of the poet.

R. Nemo Hill, "The View from The Bar" from *The Hopkins Review*. Reprinted by permission of the poet.

Tony Hoagland, "Into the Mystery" from *The Sun*. Reprinted by permission of the poet.

Anna Maria Hong, "Yonder, a Rental" from *Ecotone*. Reprinted by permission of the poet.

Sharon Olds, "Silver Spoon Ode" from *The Nation*. Reprinted by permission of the poet.

Jacqueline Osherow, "*Tilia cordata*" from *The Antioch Review*. Reprinted by permission of the poet.

Mike Owens, "Sad Math" from *The Way Back* © 2017 by Mike Owens. Reprinted by permission of Random Lane Press.

Elise Paschen, "The Week Before She Died" from *The Nightlife* © 2017 by Elise Paschen. Reprinted by permission of Red Hen Press. Also appeared in *Virginia Quarterly Review*.

Jessica Piazza, "Bells' Knells" from *Smartish Pace*. Reprinted by permission of the poet.

Aaron Poochigian, "Happy Birthday, Herod" from *The New Criterion*. Reprinted by permission of the poet.

Ruben Quesada, "Angels in the Sun" from *The American Poetry Review*. Reprinted by permission of the poet.

Alexandra Lytton Regalado, "La Mano" from *Matria* © 2017 by Alexandra Lytton Regalado. Reprinted by permission of Black Lawrence Press. Also appeared in *Green Mountains Review*.

Paisley Rekdal, "Philomela" from *Narrative*. Reprinted by permission of the poet.

Michael Robbins, "Walkman" from *The Paris Review*. Reprinted by permission of the poet.

J. Allyn Rosser, "Personae Who Got Loose" from *Copper Nickel*. Reprinted by permission of the poet.

Mary Ruefle, "Genesis" from *Poetry*. Reprinted by permission of the poet.

Kay Ryan, "Some Transcendent Addiction to the Useless" from *Parnassus: Poetry in Review*. Reprinted by permission of the poet.

Mary Jo Salter, "We'll Always Have Parents" from *The Surveyors* © 2017 by Mary Jo Salter. Reprinted by permission of Alfred A. Knopf. Also appeared in *The Common*.

Jason Schneiderman, "Voxel" from *The Literary Review*. Reprinted by permission of the poet.

Nicole Sealey, "A Violence" from *Ordinary Beast* © 2017 by Nicole Sealey. Reprinted by permission of Ecco/HarperCollins. Also appeared in *The New Yorker*.

Michael Shewmaker, "Advent" from *The Sewanee Review*. Reprinted by permission of the poet.

Carmen Giménez Smith, "Dispatch from Midlife" from *Colorado Review*. Reprinted by permission of the poet.